Praise for
CONNECTABILITY

"Rarely has great storytelling been put to a higher purpose. Fred Steck's deep understanding of human nature must have come from a master class co-taught by Charles Darwin and Sigmund Freud. *Connectability* provocatively turns the traditional business memoir on its head, imparting skills from an astonishing career in business that are less about succeeding in business than about succeeding in life, love, happiness, and personal fulfillment. For those of us who value insights about authenticity, empathy, purpose, and leadership, Fred Steck has given us a road map that guarantees we'll find our way."

—**BILLY SHORE,** Founder and Executive Chair, Share Our Strength, No Kid Hungry

"Fred Steck is one of the world's most natural and prolific connectors. His remarkable business and life successes all have one mark in common: This man knows how to build uplifting relationships. *Connectability* shares a winning set of principles to inform and inspire even the most seasoned relationship builder. Fred's fresh perspectives reinforce the timelessness and importance of human connection—especially in a world increasingly driven by technology. The sooner you find a way to incorporate his systematic approach into your life, the sooner you will reap the benefits, personally and professionally."

—**DANNY MEYER**, Restaurateur and Author, *Setting the Table: The Transforming Power of Hospitality in Business*

"In *Connectability*, Fred Steck reminds us that in an increasingly digital and fast-paced world, the human touch remains the most powerful currency in business and in life. Drawing on decades of personal experience across finance, hospitality, and sport, Fred distills timeless lessons about empathy, presence, and authentic connection. His storytelling is heartfelt and deeply relatable, providing valuable insights for professionals at any stage of their journey. As an educator and university leader, I have seen firsthand how the strongest careers and communities are built not on transactions, but on trust. Fred Steck's book is a compelling and timely guide for rediscovering that truth."

—**HENRY T. YANG**, Chancellor Emeritus and Professor of Mechanical Engineering, University of California at Santa Barbara

"It's rare to come across someone who has reached Fred Steck's level of success and can still stop and examine the world around him—and the people around him—to uncover what more he can learn. In *Connectability*, Fred reminds readers of both the power and motivation we possess within ourselves, and also shows that the key to success is often not something you need to search for or tirelessly train to learn. Instead, you need to ask the right questions and use the tools that are inherent to you. In a time when we are so quick to turn to screens, search engines, and digital intelligence, *Connectability* reminds us to look up—and offers a path to success that is tangible and human. Success is measured, in part, by those with whom you fill your life."

—**DAISY RYAN,** Co-founder, Co-owner, Companion Hospitality, Michelin Star chef, and James Beard Award Winner

CONNECTABILITY

CONNECTABILITY

Mastering Relationship Building
in Business, Sales, and Beyond

FREDRIC STECK

FAST
COMPANY
Press

This publication is designed to provide accurate and authoritative information in regard to the subject matter covered. It is sold with the understanding that the publisher and author are not engaged in rendering legal, accounting, or other professional services. Nothing herein shall create an attorney-client relationship, and nothing herein shall constitute legal advice or a solicitation to offer legal advice. If legal advice or other expert assistance is required, the services of a competent professional should be sought.

Fast Company Press
New York, New York
www.fastcompanypress.com

Copyright © 2025 Fredric Steck

All rights reserved.

Thank you for purchasing an authorized edition of this book and for complying with copyright law. No part of this book may be reproduced, stored in a retrieval system, used for training artificial intelligence technologies or systems, or transmitted by any means, electronic, mechanical, photocopying, recording, or otherwise, without written permission from the copyright holder.

Grateful acknowledgment is made to the following for permission to reproduce copyrighted material:

Hal Leonard, LLC: Lyrics from "Closing Time." Words and music by Lyle Pearce Lovett. Copyright © 1986 by Michael H. Goldsen, Inc. and Lyle Lovett Music. All Rights Reserved. Used by Permission.

This work is being published under the Fast Company Press imprint by an exclusive arrangement with *Fast Company*. *Fast Company* and the *Fast Company* logo are registered trademarks of Mansueto Ventures, LLC. The Fast Company Press logo is a wholly owned trademark of Mansueto Ventures, LLC.

Distributed by Greenleaf Book Group

For ordering information or special discounts for bulk purchases, please contact Greenleaf Book Group at PO Box 91869, Austin, TX 78709, 512.891.6100.

Design and composition by Greenleaf Book Group and Jonathan Lewis
Cover design by Greenleaf Book Group and Jonathan Lewis
Cover image used under license from ©Adobestock.com/dimj

Publisher's Cataloging-in-Publication data is available.

Print ISBN: 978-1-63908-157-8

eBook ISBN: 978-1-63908-158-5

To offset the number of trees consumed in the printing of our books, Greenleaf donates a portion of the proceeds from each printing to the Arbor Day Foundation. Greenleaf Book Group has replaced over 50,000 trees since 2007.

Printed in the United States of America on acid-free paper

25 26 27 28 29 30 31 32   10 9 8 7 6 5 4 3 2 1

First Edition

*To my amazing children—
Amanda, Abigail, Alexander, Emily, and William—
to whom I am forever and deeply connected.
Love, Dad*

Contents

Introduction 1
Chapter 1: Empathy 19
Chapter 2: Listening 31
Chapter 3: Passion 45
Chapter 4: Risk 57
Chapter 5: Creativity and Knowledge 71
Chapter 6: Present and Available 85
Chapter 7: Leadership 97
Chapter 8: Generosity 109
Chapter 9: Follow-Up 121
Chapter 10: Vulnerability 135
Chapter 11: Bringing It All Together 145
Afterthought Number 1 167
Afterthought Number 2 171
Notes 177
About the Author 181
Acknowledgments 183

Introduction

Many years ago, I sat on a bench with my childhood friends waiting to see if we had made the tennis team. Together, we were discussing what we would each become when we graduated. Of all the potential occupations mentioned, I cannot remember any of us saying we wanted to be a salesperson—or, more accurately put, a relationship builder. Yet little did we know that no matter what occupation we chose, we would all find ourselves in the business of building relationships. We would all find ourselves participating in the continuous human cycle of seeking to convince and influence others.

For me, building better relationships became the cornerstone of a long and successful career spent mostly in sales and trading at Goldman Sachs. I learned a number of essential relationship lessons through my work, as I also did through my time training and competing in the world of cutting horses. In this book, I'll draw primarily upon my experiences in both of these areas, as well as observations from another vista entirely—restaurants. You might ask: How are horses, restaurants, and sales and trading connected? The answer is: relationship building.

Success in these three vocations—along with success in relationship building in our personal lives—requires a mastery of the deeply human qualities discussed in the following pages.

There is nothing more satisfying than a relationship that moves from one successful outcome to the next. A relationship bigger than any one single transaction. A reciprocal relationship that brings significant value to each party. Relationships like this take work, and cultivating them requires attention and dedication. There is not one app on your phone or one AI message generator that is going to give you the magic tool you can use to build them. Meaningful, lasting relationships that fuel a powerful career and rich life are the result of drawing upon your deepest human powers that go beyond digital technology.

That said, this is not an anti-technology book. This is, however, a deeply pro-human book. After a forty-year career in financial services and sales, and several more years as a human living on this planet, I can tell you that the most important tool in your relationship-building tool kit (both personal and professional) is you. You—your face, your mind, your body, your heart; these are the tools that will bring success in building rewarding human relationships.

Introduction

Today, our society is rife with digital tools at our fingertips to help us communicate with others, which can be amazing communication catalysts. However, my success in cultivating meaningful, successful relationships did not come through digital tools. It was, instead, developed through a decades-long discipline centered on cultivating skills around deep human connection. By combining these skills with our digital assets, we can achieve greater success in sales through the development of enduring, strong relationships.

This book is my offering to you. A guide, if you will, to rediscovering your humanity and using it as your greatest personal and professional strength. To cultivate what is aspirational and transform it into your own innate superpower!

Today, we're in danger of losing a lot in this space of human connection. Our connective skills are starting to atrophy. We'd often rather look at our screens than at each other, and communicate through the filters that build in distance and ask less of us. As they ask less of us, though, they also give less in return. Relationships are built between people, and if you want to build well, you have to bring your humanity. Remember the human traits that are most important to you when interacting with another human or building a working relationship. These are the same important elements that will enhance your ability to succeed. In virtually any instance, your humanity more than your software is what will build great business or personal connections.

The basic weakness of digital communication is the inability to properly express your intent and feelings—emojis can only do so much. Digital allows for broad interpretation on the part of the reader, and the receiver's takeaway may not align with the writer's intention.

Simply relying on your digital tool kit and surface-level (or screen- and text-level) connection is the equivalent of walking into a restaurant, avoiding eye contact, and after placing your order, putting on headphones and staring at your phone. This might sound great to many people, but I promise you, you're not going to have a high-quality experience. Just like you're not going to have the same success in sales if you think that reaching out to hundreds of people with a canned, digitally created message is going to do the trick. You might have some success, but when people have a choice, they will almost always go with a person they like, trust, and feel most connected to in a genuine way. Real, lasting relationships are still the most fertile ground for success in sales, and these always require the human element.

My hope is that this book will serve to empower you to lean in and further develop these innate human skills already well within your being, to deepen and enrich your life and relationships around you. I want to emphasize their importance and show you how to put them into active, engaged practice. Show you how to use them as pillars in building successful long-term relationships—pillars of bringing your empathetic self, following up, listening, asking questions, and actively doing the things you most like to receive when you are with another human being.

Seeing someone's name flash on your screen, without seeing the expressions crossing their face or hearing

Introduction

the texture and tone of their voice, does not create the level of connection you need to reach your highest career aspirations—or have a deep life to savor on every level.

Success comes through deepening your connection with the person right in front of you, who can hear your voice, see your body language, and understand the sincerity of that very unique human characteristic of in-person communication.

I care about and understand the human element of sales because my own work relied on it. As a pre-IPO partner at Goldman Sachs, my success was the result of embracing curiosity and my desire to connect with others. Yet I certainly didn't begin my career as a partner. And I didn't begin my career with those skills fully developed. Far from it.

I had to learn the hard way how important these interpersonal skills were when my sales journey first began, upon arriving at my first job on Wall Street at A. G. Becker. Becker was a Chicago-based investment banking firm with a specialty in commercial paper. This was the 1970s, and at the time, the market for commercial paper was around $40 billion (today that market exceeds $1.1 trillion), and underwriting was dominated by A. G. Becker, Goldman Sachs, and Lehman Brothers.

In the months prior, I had just been released from military service in the US Army Reserve and moved to San Francisco, where A. G. Becker had recently opened an office. After multiple interviews, I was hired by the firm and found myself at a desk in the Bank of America Center,

CONNECTABILITY

with a Golden Gate–to–Bay Bridge view. I was amazed at myself for having landed such a job.

A few weeks went by and then the manager of the office, Malcolm Skall, called me in for a meeting. Malcolm was a Midwesterner who grew up on the Chicago Board of Trade and had been sent out to open the San Francisco office for the firm. He was, in a two-word phrase, "old school." Malcolm had a system for remembering birthdays, and routinely searched *The Wall Street Journal* for articles related to clients of the firm and in particular people he had a relationship with. He was disciplined, thoughtful, and sincere. To his clients and colleagues, he outwardly demonstrated that he had empathy and genuine concern for them.

I was intimidated by him, as I was not nearly as organized and had not yet developed the skills necessary to demonstrate a genuine interest in a wide range of clients with diverse requirements and goals.

As I stepped into his office, a wave of anxiety swept over me. It turned out, I had good reason for it.

"How's it going?" he asked me, in a seemingly curious fashion.

"Great," I said, a poorly thought-out answer based on what was about to come. Malcolm proceeded to ask me if I had sold anything yet. He clearly knew the answer.

Nonetheless, I was forced to answer that no, I had not sold anything, adding I was prepared to, and in the meantime, I was helping my colleagues and talking to the traders in New York. Suffice it to say, the rest of the meeting did not go well, but when I left his office, I still had a job.

Introduction

It was a job with new rules. (Rules I was not happy about. But as time marched on, I would realize their value in developing and maintaining relationships, which in turn improved my sales ability.) Malcolm explained that he and I would meet on Monday and develop a list of clients to call on, and then on Friday we would review the list to see what calls I had completed and how I would rate the prospects.

"What if I cannot get an appointment?" I asked.

"Then you will go by their office and leave your card so you can follow up at a later date," he informed me. The last bit of job reformulation was that I was not allowed in the office except on Monday and then again on Friday for our client prospect review.

I remember taking the train home that afternoon thinking there must be something wrong because this all sounded like I was a door-to-door salesman, not an investment banker. I felt jilted, and instead of doing what Malcolm had asked, I squandered my time for the next week. This was not my best job performance, especially as I was married with a child on the way.

The evening before my first Friday meeting with Malcolm, I came to a moment of understanding. I had been feeling resentful at being thrust into such a sales-heavy role, yet I realized that sales is a universal exercise, a part of virtually every relational activity. We are in a constant cycle of convincing people to either see it our way or understand our thinking and how we came to our conclusion.

I had violated many of the principles that we'll come to discuss in the following chapters. I had not bothered to understand my boss's thinking and thus was not empathetic. I was thinking only of me and not Malcolm's business framework. I hadn't listened to his instructions in a way that would inform me to take the appropriate action. Finally, I definitely did not follow up—neither on the project I was assigned nor the promise I had made.

Believing that forgiveness might be an option, I threw myself on the mercy of the court and explained to Malcolm why I had failed, but more importantly, why I would not fail again. He showed me the value of consistency and the development of relationship when he agreed to give me a second chance, even when there appeared to be no immediate reward from his perspective.

Continuing with our weekly meetings, Malcolm and I developed a new group of potential clients he thought would be valuable to call on. They were all in what was then considered Savings and Loans. But before I made a call, I was required to research the industry and the institutions within it.

Malcolm understood the clients he was covering, not only diligently making sure he was well informed on the issues facing an industry, but also remembering its important events and benchmarks, along with personal milestones. Even the inconsequential got noticed—he never forgot a birthday. His empathetic nature was demonstrated daily, and he continually educated himself to keep on top of his clients' business. He never let things slip by, and this consistent, knowledgeable approach told his clients he cared about them and he cared about their business.

Introduction

I tried to emulate this behavior as I was building my own client base. As I worked through the list of clients we had put together, one client in Los Angeles stood out from the rest. This client responded well to my calls and was willing to discuss ideas and markets, although there seemed to be very little reward for me from a business standpoint. I continued to cultivate the relationship, along with others, striving to make my growing list of clients—even ones small in terms of revenue—feel valued and important to me and the firm. Then one day just before Christmas, my LA client's company was purchased for cash, and he needed to invest the proceeds immediately. As it happened, the eventual trade was one of the largest for the firm and the developing secondary market in certificates of deposit. This business event was a hallmark for my career.

I had initially struggled with the realization that my business was in fact sales, but following my and Malcolm's "readjustment" meeting and the creation of my developing client list, I became comfortable with my role as a salesman and began to actively cultivate sales skills, learning as much as I could from Malcolm. By the time of my Christmas transaction, I had come to understand the value of these lessons.

The actual dollar amount of the transaction was $200 million, which was many times anything I had done previously. It was not necessarily competitive. I was my client's only call. But the question is, how was I able to build this deep relationship with this client, enough so that when he had a large investment to make, I was his only call?

CONNECTABILITY

I've spent considerable time pondering this question, and the answer goes beyond this particular client to encompass all my success in sales throughout my career. The answer has become what I think of as essential building blocks to relationship development in sales: empathy, listening, passion, risk, creativity and knowledge, being present and available, leadership, generosity, follow-up, and vulnerability. These are all principles that at a human level deepen and cement the foundation of a productive relationship. They are human qualities we all possess and can develop. They require no programming or equipment. However, they do require consistency of thought, creativity, and performance.

My year-end success with this account marked the beginning of a very successful career in financial services. After my early years at A. G. Becker, I was fortunate enough to have an opportunity at Goldman Sachs. Making use of these building block principles, I was able to grow rich relationships with clients and colleagues, and eventually came to manage over four hundred salespeople in the United States for the firm.

In looking back, I believe it was the tenets that Malcolm insisted upon that helped me understand the basics of relationship development and sales, which are all human centered. In many respects the tenets now seem so old school, yet they work. Malcolm never forgot a client's important events. He never forgot to follow up on requests. He was consistent and knowledgeable. His clients knew that through him they had access to every level of the firm,

Introduction

and therefore, if he did not know the answer, they knew he would find it for them. Clients felt like more than a means to an end; they felt cared for.

Technology will not stand still and the tools will change. I was fortunate to learn and to make use of technology as it changed and grew, and I know if we use these tools wisely, they can be powerful aids. Long gone are the days when technology played a small role in building relationships. Yet we need to balance the use of tech with awareness and discipline around the simple principles of human interaction that are still so vital:

- Empathy
- Listening
- Passion
- Risk
- Creativity and knowledge
- Being present and available
- Leadership
- Generosity
- Follow-up
- Vulnerability

All simple concepts, but they can be revolutionary when consistently utilized and actively engaged. And while there's nothing revolutionary about the above terms themselves, there's a power in weaving them together into your business building. This is not commonly done. In the digital age, it's being done less and less. As a culture, we're becoming

CONNECTABILITY

more comfortable with less connection. Yet connection is always the foundation.

One of the best illustrations of the power of real human connection can be found in the world of restaurants, and to me, this is shown most notably at one of my favorite restaurants: Bell's. Bell's is situated in a single-street, Central California town, Los Alamos, known more for its "biker bar" than for fine dining. Ten years ago, you would have either driven by the town if you blinked or would have stopped only if you were desperate for gas. Yet here, in this small, conservative steak-and-potatoes town, a young couple opened a restaurant, which against all odds became a Michelin Star French bistro.

Daisy Ryan had graduated from the Culinary Institute of America. She met her husband, Greg, in NYC while working at Per Se. They lived there ten years, then LA for a year, and then moved to Texas for three years. He was interested in restaurants and the growing farm-to-table movement that had taken root in culinary circles, and with Daisy's culinary abilities, they decided to return to Daisy's hometown of Santa Ynez—where I lived for a number of years—and establish a restaurant of their own. Now that I live farther north, I don't get to visit quite as often, but it's always close in my memory. It's not the sort of place you forget, and I'm not saying that only because of the food. It's mainly because of the relationships I built there.

Every time I walked into Bell's, I was greeted with real warmth. When seated, the servers took their time as I asked questions. They shared their detailed knowledge of the food

Introduction

and wine with a richness the printed menu alone could never convey. They felt like friends, as did the owners. In fact, the owners became such good friends that I eventually traveled with them to Europe on a dining tour. Because of this deep human connection that extended through all aspects of the experience, dining at Bell's was incredible.

I am, of course, interested in the food a restaurant has to offer—but in many ways, it's more of a given that an excellent restaurant will present a high-quality food product.

What's more intriguing and valuable to me, both as a customer and someone who found significant success in sales, is the development of the relationship between those orchestrating the experience and the client.

Restaurants encapsulate the human desire to connect on a personal level, which is why the best of them illustrate the best of relationship building within sales. In this environment, the server acts as the salesperson, the conduit between the product in the kitchen and its presentation to the client. In one brief interlude (or many), the server can demonstrate a level of connection that can bring the client closer to what the restaurant offers, and build loyalty in the process.

Bell's, like other successful, memorable restaurants, offers a simple and incredible example of the power of deep, long-term relationship building. We can look at this power of human connection further, though, by flipping to the other side of the table: to the customer or client. Because just as the best restaurants are building relationships as they sell, customers also have the chance to demonstrate something

CONNECTABILITY

pretty game-changing—a desire to engage in the depth of experience at hand, through engaging with the person in front of them. For human beings, this desire can open up a beautiful, full life. And for salespeople, this can also open up new levels of success.

When a server approaches your table, you can treat them simply as a functionary—a means to an end, which is your food. Or you can, instead, engage with your server with curiosity, experiencing them as the multifaceted person they are, one who also holds more knowledge of the available food and flavors than you do. There is so much to be curious about when you walk into a restaurant; there's a story behind everything. You can engage with your server with real interest, then listen. The more you listen, ask questions, and demonstrate a degree of interest in what the server says, the more rewarding your experience.

There is nothing so enriching as the opportunity to exchange information and learn something about other people and ideas in the world, beyond the bare minimum we need to get us to our chosen end point. Generally, we care about the outcomes too. Yet when we approach the journey to what we want with curiosity and a desire to connect, we usually reach a better end point. This means everything in sales.

Sales comes down to connection, which comes down to fundamental human qualities that our current digital world isn't helping us to adequately develop. In-person communication, or as near to it as possible, still matters. While we currently still have waitstaff in restaurants, as a

Introduction

society we're moving toward less human connectivity in a multitude of other ways. We order delivery at the tap of a screen. In comparison, even a phone call to order our pizza can feel like too much work and interaction. Maybe we even feel the same way about our friends. Why call when a quick text will suffice? And in our work, we reach out digitally as our suite of tools enables us—which is great. As the sophistication of digital communication continues to grow, it will become an even more essential form of communication. However, it is only one of many tools we should use when communicating with others.

Although it feels safer to text a message, and keep any potential rejection further away from us, the distance of texting comes at its own risk. We lose body language, tone of voice, inflection, eye contact, and facial expression—all nuances that add to the value and true meaning of your communication. Digital communication cannot provide the qualities that the human body and mind are meant to receive and interpret. This truth, which most of us can feel intuitively, is also supported by research. In October of 2023, Yale neuroscientist Joy Hirsch completed a study that found "neural signaling during online exchanges was substantially suppressed compared to activity observed in those having face-to-face conversations."[1] "In an article reviewed by Danielle Ellis, B.Sc., Hirsch is quoted as saying, "These findings illustrate how important live, face-to-face interactions are to our natural social behaviors."[2]

Other studies suggest that part of the reason we tire so quickly of video calls is the body is spending time and

CONNECTABILITY

energy trying to interpret that static and unnuanced communication delivered over a digital platform.[3] What it points to is simply this: We are not built electronically, and thus our brain and body struggle to interpret what they were not built to understand.

Despite their comparative ineffectiveness, people are growing more comfortable with the digital forms of communication that diminish relational depth. That's going to make them less effective as salespeople, and also, I would argue, less effective in life. I am not throwing digital platforms out the window in exchange for the "good old days" of analog. However, I would like to establish the necessity of developing fundamental human qualities that promote deeper connection and to offer guidance toward doing so. It's through the combination of analog and digital that we can achieve greater success in sales and the further development of enduring and meaningful relationships.

Interestingly enough, a recent survey by Deloitte found that workers believe they need people skills more than tech skills but that their employers value tech skills more. Workers across generations seek more help in developing enduring human capabilities than technical capabilities. Those surveyed believe that training in human skills has fallen short and that these skills are necessary for career advancement.[4]

For each of the principles discussed in this book, I will include my own experience cultivating each element and seeing its impact. They are not all stories from business but rather draw upon my interpersonal experiences throughout

Introduction

my life; these experiences include some failures as well as successes. Good leaders find both to be essential in learning, growing, and teaching.

As you read through these next chapters, think how you can apply these principles on a daily basis. It's more difficult than you may think and requires thoughtful focus, but as you integrate each one more and more, they will become a part of how you relate to people. How you connect.

Connection is at the heart of this book, and so in choosing a title, I explored the etymology behind the word. Connection builds upon "connect," which began with the fifteenth century Latin "conectere," meaning "to join together." In French, this became "connexer," which in 1881 became the familiar word "connecter."

These evolving words hold the meanings "to join together," "to establish a relationship with," and "to awaken meaningful emotions, establish rapport." I drew upon these root meanings to inform the title, a word that for me holds echoes of our modern ability to connect with ease and also these historical notes of deep meaning.

Through reading this book, I hope you can grow in connectability—to become someone who not only utilizes the easy forms of connection all around us when appropriate, but also cultivates relationships that go deeper. When you bring attention to this, again and again, your relationship to the world itself changes.

You will become someone who, for example, is more genuinely curious about what your server might have to say to you when dining at a restaurant. You'll more and

CONNECTABILITY

more appreciate those moments of possible connection and what they offer. And as you open to greater success in sales, you'll also open to greater richness in all your life.

The depth of what is possible depends on the depth and openness you bring to it. And so, let's begin.

CHAPTER 1

Empathy

Growing up in New York City, my son William hated running around on the soccer field. To fix this problem he decided to play goalie. But being goalie on a team of six-year-olds was not very exciting, and as a result, he wasn't enthusiastic about the sport. Then he went to an ice skating birthday party at Wollman Rink in Central Park. After a few more trips, he discovered he could go a lot faster on skates than he could running. Putting on skates was truly a life-altering experience for him, as hockey has become foundational for his life.

This early discovery of ice hockey, alongside his natural tendency to be highly empathetic, would determine the path of his career and future success.

CONNECTABILITY

Hockey is a bit of a cult sport. If you are proficient at it, you are part of a small fraternity of players, especially if you play at a high level, which William did. He also, on top of his "day job," coaches the University of Denver men's club hockey team. Good coaches and players live and breathe the sport and the team. William is a good coach. He took over from a staff that did not bring their truly authentic selves, but once he joined the team, they began to see greater success. They now attend year-end playoffs and championships on a regular basis.

More than coaching success on the ice, William is truly interested in every one of his players—not only on the surface but also on a deeper level filled with empathy and caring. He makes the effort to know his players beyond their hockey skills. He is interested in the whole of the player—how they grew up, their goals and aspirations, and their workload at the university. All of this understanding helps him as a coach and mentor for these young men. The following is a story that exemplifies his empathetic, whole-person attitude.

One evening, one of his players became quite ill. The player's family lived in Philadelphia, and being alone and in distress he called William, his coach, to ask what he should do. William escorted him to the hospital and helped him get admitted and then called his parents in Philadelphia to explain the situation. The parents immediately booked the next flight to Denver. As the parents wouldn't arrive for many hours, William made the decision to stay with this young man until they arrived. After staying at the hospital all night and knowing his player had stabilized,

Empathy

William left to pick up the boy's mother and bring her to the hospital. After the parents and young man were united, and the mother had been introduced to the hospital staff, William returned home. It turned out the young man had a severe case of mononucleosis that had impacted his liver. He successfully recovered from this incident. The young man's parents wrote to the university to express their gratitude at how their son's club hockey coach had gone above and beyond to help their son.

Your choice of moving through life can be either insular or inclusive. The narrow silo approach is to keep your concern within your own narrow boundaries. Life as a snapshot is limited; make sure you fit your camera with a wide-angle lens.

In the story above, both the approach and outcome could have been very different. William could have given some advice and let the player find a solution on his own, and the outcome could have been more dire. We see people taking action like this everywhere—ignoring a problem or assuming someone else will step in to solve it, being self-absorbed and interacting with others in a more transactional style.

William's approach, on the other hand, is to be a participant rather than an observer. Going beyond the bare minimum expected. His empathy is natural but also intentional and has benefited not only others in his life but also himself and his business relationships.

When we lived in New York, William, his sister Emily, and I would often go to a small French restaurant on the

CONNECTABILITY

Upper East Side called Le Bilboquet. It was one of those "you have to know about it" restaurants. I was never sure whether they even had a published phone number. Certainly, there was no sign on the door. Le Bilboquet became very well known to the three of us. We would go there for dinner on Sunday evenings, and as the people who ran the restaurant got to know us, it became an event for everyone. This establishment moved from being merely a restaurant to a place that became part of our family fabric. It added a layer to each evening as we shared a meal. Our interaction with each other and with the people in the restaurant meant more to us than the food.

Many years later, William was working for the Fritz Knoebel School of Hospitality Management at the University of Denver. One morning he read in the local paper that Le Bilboquet was opening a restaurant in the tonier Cherry Creek area of Denver. Could it be that this restaurant that had added an important layer to his NYC life would actually be opening in Denver? he wondered. He placed a call to the number listed in the newspaper article, and when he reached the manager who was hiring and setting up the restaurant for the opening, he introduced himself. William explained that he worked for the University of Denver and suggested this new restaurant might want to have a relationship with the school. William offered to provide an introduction to the dean of the school.

The manager did have a sincere interest in being introduced to the university. The restaurant business can be transitory, and having access to a potential worker pool is

Empathy

important. Especially if that pool of potential employees is already interested in hospitality. The University of Denver is one of the top hospitality schools in the US, and having access would be an asset. The manager was curious how William had come to think of them and make this call, and asked if he would meet with them at the new restaurant. They were impressed with his story of growing up in New York City and frequenting their establishment on the Upper East Side. They were also impressed with his understanding of their needs and demonstration of empathetic thinking.

This creative and empathetic thinking led to William being offered the job as maître d' for the restaurant when it opened. William was of course surprised, as this was not his intention. Without experience, offering him such an important job for a sophisticated new restaurant was nothing short of amazing. To me, it made perfect sense.

The owners of Le Bilboquet recognized how well William would present himself as knowledgeable and sincere when dealing with patrons of the restaurant, because he had demonstrated such authentic interest in them first. Empathy is not just being smooth and charming. It is not about agreeing on everything or getting what you want. It goes deeper than that. It's about the authenticity that touches people when you are sincerely extending yourself, to either understand them more or create a solution. The functionary skills of a job such as maître d' can easily be taught. A more important skill to ensure success in the hospitality business is one's ability to be empathetic and demonstrate a willingness to understand another's needs and motivation.

The epilogue to this story: Working as maître d' at the newest restaurant in town gave William the opportunity to meet many of the important people in Denver. Having a job that exposes you to others who might have an interest in hiring you is a high-value job, and indeed, that came to pass. The owner of an important insurance brokerage agency offered William an opportunity to change careers into a new professional area, which suited him exceptionally well.

I am sure that William was hired there in the same way that he was hired without experience at Le Bilboquet. The owners of both companies recognized his profound desire and ability to be empathetic.

The abilities that help make your customers feel welcomed at a restaurant are the same as in any business where you are building a working relationship—the ability to extend a genuine interest in your clients; the ability to demonstrate empathy when problem-solving; the ability to be authentic and interested in making sure your clients are happy, even if they did not get the exact table they wanted. Being obsequious with false charm is not empathetic behavior. Empathetic connection is felt differently. It comes from demonstrating an authentic interest in the people you meet and work with.

To be truly empathetic means to bring your authentic self to the conversation and to sincerely try to understand the other person's point of view. This goal is challenging

Empathy

and requires focus, especially if it doesn't come naturally. It is critical for me to understand your point of view. How can I convince you to see my point of view if I do not first understand yours and the circumstances that helped you form it?

The willingness and ability to understand the person across from you are at the core of relationship development, in your personal life and sales. The more you can understand background, motivation, and desire, the better you will be able to provide the valuable service you have come to present.

As important as empathy is, we often walk through life selfishly focused on our own issues and our own success. We also tend to put people into categories when we meet them, determining value immediately and often storing them as of no interest to us. We're not always patient enough to find the value that's there.

In a business sense, our mental framework is usually to classify people as to whether or not they are a potential sale. When we meet someone outside of our immediate sphere of influence or concern, we may be polite but generally fail to make an effort to find out who they are. And in doing so, we lose the opportunity to file that understanding away for future reference.

There are those who, like William, simply have a natural ability to be empathetic. They have an innate curiosity to understand and attune to others. Like many talented athletes, they seem to come with their skill, which mentors help to refine and further develop. Many women especially tend to excel at this. (And if you already do, please never feel you must disconnect from it in order to succeed. This is truly a superpower.)

Empathy is easily articulated but far more difficult to perform, as it is hard to get out of our own way and our own desires. You don't need to be naturally skilled in this way to grow empathetically. Empathetic skills grow through intention and discipline. A good exercise is to immediately think of clarifying questions you can ask of a new acquaintance. These simple questions will send the message that you are interested and care to know more.

My hope in this book is to draw attention to the importance of empathy, and encourage you to discipline yourself to focus on this critical need in the development of relationships.

As humans we all have a natural ability to be curious about others. We're hardwired to be inquisitive and have a thirst for new information, which links back to survival for our ancestors.[1] If you don't currently have a well-developed ability to be empathetic, the first step to changing that is being aware that you have room to grow and having the desire and intention to grow. From here, you can cultivate a discipline that will help you develop new habits. You can develop a practice around getting out of your own headspace and getting inquisitive about someone else's space. I still need to remind myself to do this.

When I was recently in Italy, I found myself in a grocery store with a cashier who clearly hated her job. She looked straight past me with a blank stare as she moved me through

Empathy

the transaction. "*Puoi darmi un sacco per favore,*" I said, asking for a bag.

Without moving her gaze, and with a "Steph Curry without-looking-behind-the-back pass," she threw a plastic bag in my direction. Without acknowledging my existence as a human or a customer, she moved the few items I was purchasing through the scanner and then to me to bag up. Once, I might have thought this treatment was saved for me or perhaps other people who looked like me. But contrary to this mistaken belief, in Italy this is normal behavior. There is often no *"buongiorno,"* no *"prego,"* no "thanks for bagging," no "have a nice day."

I felt a little cheeky about this unique behavior until I eventually had lunch with some friends and brought up this topic. It was suggested I might hate my job too if I was only making one thousand euros a month. I found that hard to believe—not that I would hate the job, but that she was only making one thousand euros a month. I did a little statistical research, and I found the average wage in Italy is about 1,900 euros a month or around $24,000 a year. Sure, they also have government health care and other benefits, but that still can't be enough to live on in a G8 country in the twenty-first century. No wonder she hates her job.

When I was met with such treatment, my first reaction was to complain about it. It took me some time—with a gentle reminder from a friend—to instead view the interaction with more empathy. I find myself often needing to return back to empathy when I may have initially embodied something else. It's a continual practice that is worth the effort.

CONNECTABILITY

Empathy is all about extending beyond yourself, beyond the tunnel vision of yourself and how something is impacting you, and beyond your comfort zone. It's about allowing yourself to be a bit vulnerable. Taking the time to be thoughtful about your intentions when setting out to develop a relationship. This may sound more personal than business-oriented, but in reality they are one and the same. Those same skills that help with your personal relationship development will serve you well in your business. Taking the risk to be less guarded in your business feels like taking more risk, but it is actually opening the conversation; sincerity and slight vulnerability make you more genuine. People would always rather deal with someone who is being authentic instead of scripted.

All relationships come down to trust. Demonstrating your genuine interest and being willing to peel away part of your personal onion will establish a different kind of relationship compared to the competition. Share of yourself. But if you catch yourself talking for a long time, stop and pivot to the person you're speaking with.

An excellent exercise to build a more multilayered relationship and become more empathetically aware is to ask questions. You do not have to nor are you expected to know all the answers. This is especially true with any new relationship. That's how we learn more about the other person or institution. That's how we learn about their background and motivations.

Knowing these things, we can soon discover the needs they want to meet and the goals they want to achieve. We

Empathy

can also come to understand their perceived impediments to achieving those goals. These questions and answers will open doors to more and different sources of business and understanding. Moreover, if we do not ask any questions, the message we are signaling is a lack of interest. Asking questions will drive you down an empathetic road and will indicate to your audience that you are sincerely interested in their opinion.

Consistently engaging in relationships this way requires discipline—the discipline of getting out of your own headspace and thinking in a long-term rather than a transactional way. The desire to make the sale is a strong motivator to prove that you have already established a working relationship. However, understanding more about your client and their needs may lead to diversification of business rather than a quick sale. You can never make on one transaction what a long-term relationship can yield. A relationship that is multilayered is filled with opportunity, and thinking empathetically—taking the time to understand your client more and more—will lead you down that path.

We cannot get to know anyone well in the short term. So we should extend our vision. Rather than focusing on the immediate transaction, we then think about multiple transactions over time.

A first meeting always appears bigger than it is. In business there's a tendency to want to make a sale or at a minimum make sure the client knows the wide array of products and services you have to offer. If it's personal, we want to sell them on us—as someone they want in their life. We often see it as the make-or-break moment to make something happen, which can make it harder to ground ourselves in empathy.

The reality is the chances of making a sale on the first meeting are pretty low. The goal of the first meeting should simply be to introduce yourself, learn more about the person in front of you, and get a second meeting.

Demonstrating your ability to be empathetic, then, is a valuable asset that will help you gain the second meeting. Success in this will allow you to bring more detail to the relationship and in subsequent meetings allow you to make the sale, whether it be a product or service. From here, you can continue to approach the relationship with empathy, and the experience becomes more layered, nuanced, and interesting. You'll have the chance for relationships to deepen and possibilities to expand.

All of this, though, requires you to listen: listening for the answers to your questions, listening for the things you need to follow up on, and of course listening for what your client needs and cares about.

Let's explore the habit of listening in the next chapter.

CHAPTER 2

Listening

In the early stages of my career, I was assigned the California State Treasurer's Office. I was slightly intimidated, as this was a big responsibility for a salesman with limited experience.

I had secured an initial appointment with the treasurer's office in Sacramento one sweltering day in August. Sacramento is blazing hot in the summer. You appeared more dedicated visiting in the summer heat than you did visiting on your way to ski in Lake Tahoe during the winter. (Believe me, accounts notice that kind of detail.)

I arrived early, excited to get started. Having done my homework, I was prepared to show the chief investment officer what my firm and I could do. I was, of course, nervous, and after our introductory pleasantries, I started immediately talking, hoping to demonstrate my capabilities and my company's broad reach. It did not occur to me to stop and ask questions. I just wanted him to know that I knew a lot and had a lot of things for him to purchase—securities, I added, that would not be available tomorrow.

When I finally stopped talking, this gentleman said to me, "I look forward to hearing from you in the days ahead, but let me offer two pieces of advice. First, take time to listen to your client, especially in the beginning, because I will tell you what securities I need. Second, I am not going to buy anything from you today even if you say they will not be available tomorrow. Because I have no doubt in my mind that you will have something for me to buy tomorrow."

This advice would prove valuable over the years. I believe that anytime you are embarking on developing a new relationship, you are intimidated by the unknown outcome of your first meeting. Talking more than you should is a natural way to hide one's feeling of intimidation and nervousness. This meeting, though, taught me a great lesson. You learn nothing if you are doing all the talking. You can't increase your knowledge when you're primarily focused on reciting it.

The art of listening is one of your most valuable tools in building and maintaining productive relationships. Through listening, you demonstrate your interest in learning what your client's thought process is and what is of value to them. Listening will be the seed that will germinate and

Listening

build successful, collaborative achievements. After all, how can I convince you of anything if I do not first understand your point of view?

After my experience with the state treasurer, I brought new attention to my level of listening, which required patience and stepping back from my own agenda. I had significant success with developing my listening skills while in sales—it became an integral part of a successful career. However, my capacity to listen grew to another level after I embarked on another chapter of training horses at a ranch I purchased in Central California.

I spent years working with a horse trainer learning how to train horses. JT was an old Idaho cowboy who had already forgotten more about horses than I would ever know. He was also a man of few words, so if you were not listening closely, you often missed the most important part of what he was saying. Horses require time and patience to train. You and they have to learn to communicate, which requires focused listening on the trainer's part because a horse is very subtle. JT was a master at patience and letting these highly sensitive animals come to him. Forcing the issue only drove them away.

Training horses with patience is a true metaphor for building relationships. Allowing your relationship target to come to you with information and problems while seeking resolution will help facilitate collaboration. They will be far more receptive to you for your critical thinking and analytical skills. I learned this over and over again in my time training horses.

CONNECTABILITY

JT and I specialized in training two-year-old horses, preparing them for serious competition. The breed we worked with was the traditional Western United States quarter horse, one of the oldest in the US. Dating back to the 1660s, the quarter horse is a cross between native horses of Spanish origin and English horses imported from Virginia. This is the basic cowboy horse, used extensively in ranches in the West. We were training horses for the performance horse competition known as cutting, an event that requires smooth teamwork between horse and rider as they execute different skills in perfect coordination.

Training horses is not as often depicted in Western movies. It's a slow, iterative process that begins with getting the horse comfortable with the basic tools and equipment needed for a human to sit astride a massive animal—first a halter and then progressing to a hackamore, blanket, and saddle. Introducing this equipment requires time and patience to allow the horse to grow comfortable enough so a rider can then climb aboard.

As in my sales career, I had a lot to learn, and this time from JT. My listening, and patience, developed in new and rewarding directions. As these animals are highly sensitive, you have to be too in order to be a successful trainer. As an example, a basic accomplishment is having the young colt accept you placing a blanket on its back for the first time. The morning you begin blanket training, you start by putting the horse in a paddock and entering with a blanket in hand. If you're lucky, the young horse allows you to place the blanket on its back, and the lesson is over. More than

Listening

likely, though, this lesson will take time and commitment. You cannot leave until you have achieved your goal. A horse doesn't understand that you have a conference call to attend after an hour of trying to get the blanket on its back. If you leave, you have taught the horse that it does not have to accept the blanket. Therefore, once you are in the paddock, you are there until you are successful. That requires patience. It also requires you to "listen" to what the horse is telling you. Every nuance of behavior requires your attention if you want to achieve success. You and the horse are learning to listen to each other.

Using my horse story as an analogy for relationship building, let's assume you are embarking on the initial stages of development with a new client. Think of your efforts to attempt to contact your prospective client. If you call one day and then don't attempt to call for a week because you were unsuccessful, each time you make a call you are essentially starting over. Just like each time you enter the paddock, it is a new day. The horse metaphor will serve as a reminder that you must be consistent in your efforts and, above all, you have to listen to what your client is telling you.

Listening successfully is about achieving balance between what you already know and what you are being taught. When I started working with JT, I knew a little about horses and he knew a lot. To take on this new challenge, I had to learn how to listen to the knowledge he was passing on to me. His style of talking was different than mine. My brain would fight with what it knew and what it

CONNECTABILITY

was willing to absorb while listening—if you know a little, sometimes you think you know it all and your listening brain shuts down. In a fashion, the knowledge you already possess blocks the new information you are receiving. My horse experience was a good exercise in being open to new information, which allowed me to better perform my job.

Each horse is different with a different personality and skill set. Basic knowledge is a good foundation, but you have to be open to new information that can help you achieve your goal. Real listening is not just hearing the words in your ears. It means taking in information based on your ability to pay close attention and to assimilate the information without preconceived judgment.

When you first begin to feel sick and are attentive to the changes in how you feel, you are listening to your body tell you that you are ill. With this information, you can rest and often be fully revived the next day. Ignoring what your body is saying leads to longer illness. Learning to listen to your body helps you gather information that you can use to make choices leading to a more successful outcome. In that same manner, developing our listening skills to hear what our clients and relationships are saying is analogous to listening to the nonverbal cues we receive from our bodies—and in my case from the horses I was working with.

The value of listening at this high level is that you become attentive to your clients' needs. By listening deeply, you gain the knowledge that will allow you to define and refine your approach to successfully developing that relationship, leading you to achieving your goal.

Listening

Listening isn't always easy. I remember when my children were young. Picking them up from school could be a wonderful event of the day, or if they were fighting and arguing, a miserable experience. If it was one of those days filled with disagreement, I could shut off my hearing and not be bothered by the bickering coming from the back seat. This ability to shut off the noise can be a very valuable skill if you are driving carpool. However, if we unconsciously shut off our hearing when we are either uninterested or distracted with a client, the results are not positive.

You must train yourself to stay engaged and listen, even if you feel your attention is drawn elsewhere—such as to what you have to sell. If you are focused on what you want to offer, sometimes you tune out your client without realizing it. You hear the words, but you are not absorbing them. The trick to deep listening with your full presence is to leave your agenda behind. Your focus is better in data accumulation mode and listening to the other person. Don't try to debate your client in your head. Focus on what is being said.

I've found that bringing a notepad to a meeting is an important way to keep your focus. It also says that you are engaged and interested enough to take notes. On top of this, you can always refer to these notes when it is your turn to talk and respond to what you have learned from your client. Of course, you have knowledge and experiences you wish to share, and it can be a challenge to be patient. Using notes is a great way to make sure you remember what you want to contribute and use that information at the best possible time.

CONNECTABILITY

Listening sends a powerful message. I was at a dinner recently and the person sitting across from me spent the entire dinner talking. He told me about all the famous people he knew. He filled me in on his activities and his opinions. He was telling me everything whether I needed to know it or not. When I mentioned that I had done something interesting, he pointed out he had done the same thing, only better. He had no interest in asking me a question and clearly had no interest in listening. Throughout the dinner his intense not-listening mode was sending a powerful message to me. He was not interested in me and therefore I became disengaged and uninterested in forging a productive relationship. Our relationship was going nowhere because there was no exchange in mutual listening. Because of that, the message I was receiving was that I had nothing of value. If that is the message you are delivering, it will be difficult if not impossible to develop common ground that increases value for either party. Real relationship building is a mutual exchange of listening skills.

There is an interesting tension in sales: The challenge in wanting to establish your credibility and the patience to listen. We want clients to know we have information that can be and will be valuable. While most of the time the only way to convey that is through telling them, I suggest you let them speak at first, and pay close attention to learn what the other person knows and what they do not know. In that way you can actually add value by respecting what they already know and fill in the gaps when it's your turn to speak.

Listening

I want to achieve a balance between listening and telling, so we are both being acknowledged for the things we know and are both open for the things we need to know. I want the messaging—whether direct or subtle—to clearly say: I am listening.

In my years in sales, I wanted the person sitting across from me to know that I was paying attention. In addition to listening closely, I also had a few simple tools to convey the message I was being attentive. Two of these were a pen and paper, the same tools I used to help keep my focus. You might think a notes app on a phone can achieve the same result, but I disagree. A phone can do too many other things, and I don't want my client to think I am doing anything other than listening. My pen and paper deliver a much clearer message. Your notes are for future reference for things you have promised to follow up on during the conversation. This is a simple tool to help retain and remember. Think of going to a doctor appointment and hearing all of the information that is helpful to you. It may be just me but I have trouble remembering all of the details of my appointment. I appreciate that my doctor sends me a summary of our appointment to help me remember. In this same way, simple note-taking is a handy way to retain knowledge and help you to remember what you promised to do. What is important to note is that you and your client will forget some percentage of what you present. The value of listening and effective note-taking will be a guide for future meetings and follow-up.

Asking questions is another vital aspect of listening. Just as it helps us to cultivate more empathetic and authentic relationships, it helps us understand what we're hearing and shows we are sincerely interested and paying close attention. Our teachers always encouraged us to ask questions. I am sure many of you, like me, were too embarrassed or unsure of what questions we should ask. No one wanted to be embarrassed in the classroom by asking the "dumb" question. In truth there are no dumb questions, unless perhaps asking the same one twice.

Questions of clarification will build knowledge that will help in problem-solving for clients. You are building information you can use to understand your clients' needs. Making sure you understand the information you are receiving fully allows you to find the best way to add value. This discovery leads to tasks that you can follow up on, which may lead to another chance and another meeting. Look for those opportunities to be in front of your client or the person you are convincing of your added value. Additionally, you are showing the speaker respect. Respect for them and the position they are in as the client. Listening and questioning send the clear message you are absorbing the information being given. People want to be understood and over time that attitude will be noticed and rewarded.

When it's time for you to respond and speak, consider your speaking style. A longtime business colleague of mine spoke very slowly and thoughtfully with a potential client. Several positives come from that style. His use of this style sends the clear message that he is diligent and thoughtful. When he asked a question, it was well-thought-out. He

Listening

never talked over those who were talking. He took his time and never rushed a response. The interesting thing about that style was it caused all in the room to be laser focused on the response he was making us wait for. Many of us are accustomed to trying to claim our chance to speak and therefore we're focused on the end of someone's sentence. My friend did not do that. Instead, he waited for people. His style would draw people into the conversation at his pace. They focused on him because they were waiting for him to speak. This approach led to his audience seeing him as highly intellectual and thoughtful, which underlined his comments.

Observe how people of importance listen and the manner in which they deal with conversations. Many appear uninterested, distracted, or aloof. The message they are sending is: I am so busy with other issues, and this isn't really worth my time. One person of importance I was deeply impressed with as a listener was Robert Rubin, who was co-senior partner at Goldman Sachs and later the treasury secretary under Bill Clinton. He had an amazing ability to be totally focused the entirety of a conversation. If you were in conversation with him, you felt there was nothing more important than you. (Unsurprisingly, his approach to listening is intentional. In his book *The Yellow Pad: Making Better Decisions in an Uncertain World*, he discusses leadership, along with the importance of listening and his style of doing so.)

Both of these styles focus on the person with whom you are interacting. Within the context of your own personality, it is important to be thoughtful in how you are perceived as a listener. I want people to know that I am focused on them and listening with intent. The more you present yourself as a good listener, the stronger you will be at building relationships.

Effective listening is of paramount importance in capturing the attention of those you are selling to or persuading.

Yet while we're touching on the importance of how you are perceived, it isn't all about you. In the arena of sales, you cannot be the center of attention. And that applies to your own mental attention, too.

If you behave like my acquaintance at dinner who only wanted to talk about what he knew and what he had done, you will have trouble attaining a second meeting with anyone. People might want to hear about your accomplishments, but if you make those the center of the conversation, it leaves no room for the relationship. Your client and their needs should always be the center focus. Being empathetic and listening are tools that will help you maintain this focus in a meaningful way.

You'll have to work at it to first create the opportunity to listen. Not everyone likes to talk about themselves. Yet if you want to build a relationship, it's worth trying to draw someone out. By paying attention to their voice intonation and other cues, you can recognize when you find a conversational pathway that resonates with them. While you may have your own intent for the exchange, don't hold to it too tightly; explore what lights them up. This is truly active listening.

Listening

I found that when I was training horses, active listening was incredibly important. Because horses are such sensitive creatures, you have to be attentive to their mood of the day. It may be hard to imagine, I know, but they too wake up in bad moods sometimes. (Think of a broodmare staying in a stall with a one-week-old foal who is constantly moving around, feeding, and never letting the mare relax. You would be in a bad mood too.) Rather than fighting the mood, you learn to only ask of the horse what the horse is willing to give you. Likewise, when you are speaking with a client, you never want to press for more than they are willing to give.

The idea of actively listening includes not only following—or guiding—the conversational threads in a way that helps them open up more, but also making sure you are not pushing beyond the limit of what your counterpart is willing to impart to you.

Being a good listener is the first step to achieving a positive and effective relationship.

There is more that needs to be done, though. After you have accumulated all this information, the most effective relationship builders tackle the next hard part—using the information they have absorbed in the most useful way.

This is where your digital tools can be most helpful. In fact, I prefer to gather my notes and develop a list of follow-up items in a digital format. There are many programs and formats to help you catalogue and thus better retain and follow up on the information you have attained through effective listening. Your effectiveness in sales and relationship development will depend on how well you follow up, so take this seriously. Your client or relationship target will want to work with someone who cares about their goals and business as much as they do. Listening, curiosity, and follow-up are critical in sending this message. They also indicate your passion and caring.

    I want people to understand that I care about what I am doing. Through empathy and listening, you demonstrate your passion for what you do. In the next chapter, we will explore passion and how it can be used to effectively increase the valuable relationships that you build.

CHAPTER 3

Passion

I remember my first day on the job at Goldman. I was filled with excitement, a result of my desire to excel and prove my value, and from the rush of the unfamiliar. I had a passion for my career, which drove me to excel at every task and interaction. According to *The Britannica Dictionary*, passion is "a strong feeling of enthusiasm or excitement for something or about doing something."[1] The goal in relationship building is to keep that passion alive because it energizes you and those with whom you are building relationships.

I was passionate about my business, especially the avenues that were opened to me because of it. I was filled with a sincere interest that could be felt by colleagues and clients

CONNECTABILITY

alike. Being involved in the securities markets opened the entire world to me. Markets are affected by all matter of events—whether social, political, or economic—and this constant flow of information is what makes them so fascinating.

The world around us—past, present, and future—is of deep interest to me. I was a history major in college and have always appreciated the sense of the world that a liberal arts education offered me, especially as we in the US tend not to teach history very deeply in public school—at least not in the way that European education focuses on history. When you're at a cocktail party in Venice, Italian history and how it fits into the current state of the world is just part of the conversation. Unlike, say, in California, where you might instead talk for forty minutes about the different freeway routes you took to get to the party based on what the traffic looked like. If you ever saw that *Saturday Night Live* skit "The Californians," it was spot-on.

My background in liberal arts and history didn't appear to be particularly well suited to a business that seemed to be about spreadsheets and math. But I learned investment banking wasn't just a business about mathematics. It was about understanding the world and how one might view it. If you are making investments, you want to have an understanding of what history has taught you. I became passionate about my work because I could see history playing out in real time.

At Goldman we often held conferences for central bankers. (A central bank is a financial institution given privileged

Passion

control over the production and distribution of money and credit for a nation. In modern economies, the central bank is usually responsible for the formulation of monetary policy and the regulation of member banks.) This particular conference was for central bank representatives from Central and South America, along with their counterparts from the Federal Reserve in New York. Observing these bankers from different countries at the opening reception was revealing. The bankers from Central and South America were mingling and engaging with other representatives. The New York central bankers were much more insular, talking only to each other. This observation shed light on geopolitical dynamics that went beyond banking. The citizens of Latin America live geographically closer to each other and therefore have grown accustomed to relating to each other on a more regular basis. Bankers from the US are more likely to interact with bankers from another state rather than another country with a different culture. Our size makes us more prone to be insular.

All of this was fascinating to me, as it proved that careers can be narrowly defined or can become deeper and more varied if we let our passion open other avenues of interest. It's easier for us to understand careers on the obvious, elevator-pitch level. We hear of a cowboy and think he's just about riding horses—and yes, they're passionate about riding horses, but the real passion comes from all that's involved in understanding another powerful mammal who doesn't speak English. People who work with horses are really philosophers and animal whisperers.

CONNECTABILITY

They've learned a tremendous amount of sensitivity and wisdom about life.

Likewise, it's easy to see Wall Street as the *Wolf of Wall Street* cliché, just about people making a lot of money, but there's a lot more going on below the surface. My passion for the business was multifold. True, there was the passion for making transactions, writing tickets, that immediate rush of success. I could sell $100 million of securities on my word, with my voice. It felt amazing that that was possible. Yet the larger passion for me went beyond that. Our business wasn't just a transactional entity. We were multilayered. I found my passion in many of those layers, as well as the larger function of our work in the world. The truth is investment banking provides the fuel that drives companies to grow and therefore encourages the development of our economy and our culture.

In every profession and business, there's more going on than meets the eye—and that means there are numerous places for passion to enter in. What aspects of business, even if they're not the most obvious ones on the surface, are of interest to you? What larger role in the world does your business or industry serve—is it something that feels important and valuable to you? Remember that your job is also multilayered and embedded in a greater global context. If you don't already feel passion for your work, consider these questions and try to find the points of connection. You might discover that some of the more ancillary qualities of your work light you up.

Finding a place of passion is critical to your lasting

Passion

success. I'm more compelling when I'm talking about something I truly care about, and so are you. If you don't care about your project or our relationship, why should I?

Your passion can also become the factor that removes doubt; feeling and demonstrating passion for your efforts underscores your credibility and believability. So don't be afraid to show it. The positive feedback you receive will keep the fire burning through challenges and growing familiarity with your job, product, idea, or relationship. In the broad field of commerce or the exchange of ideas or the ongoing development of a good relationship, passion for your product or idea can be what makes the crucial difference.

I'd like to now return to the story of Bell's, the French-style restaurant in a small California town more noted for steak and eggs than *steak au poivre*. The food speaks for itself: It's excellent. However, I believe that here, passion made the crucial difference. Daisy and Greg, the young couple who started this restaurant, have passion for what they do, and it allowed them to create a successful Michelin Star restaurant, and transformed the culture of the one-street town from a gas station rest stop to a sought-out culinary destination with a variety of restaurants and shops. Their dedication to hospitality and care for their employees have made their business a success, especially through challenging times like a pandemic.

A customer can feel this passion the moment they walk in the door. The enthusiasm Bell's employees bring to the table is an unmistakable indication they are cared for and treated with respect.

CONNECTABILITY

Everyone at Bell's is rowing the boat in the same direction and with shared passion for providing superior hospitality and care for their clients. Daisy and Greg are two entrepreneurs who make every guest feel that the restaurant was opened just for them. Simply put, they are dedicated to their craft. Their passion is making their business a productive enterprise for themselves, their employees, and their patrons.

Another hospitality business that combines great passion and dedication, and thus is building a loyal following, is the Post Ranch Inn in Big Sur, California. While most hotels are trying to cut costs to become more profitable, Mike Freed, the co-owner of the Post Ranch Inn, is the epitome of great management skills that draw upon passion rather than a myopic focus on the bottom line.

The Post Ranch Inn is dedicated to serving their guests with an even better product than the one they experienced on their last visit. Instead of reducing costs, Mike spends his energy making the experience better. When Covid hit, Mike spent time researching ways to make the air quality better inside than it was outside so his dining room air was safer for his guests. He remodeled rooms to improve the quality of the experience and also the safety of his guests. This is not to say Mike is inattentive to his return on his investment. The Post Ranch Inn is widely regarded as the top-ranked small inn in the US, most notably earning the title "#1 Top Hideaway in the US" in the 2025 Andrew Harper Members Choice Awards, and that brings significant success. His passion drives the

Passion

innovation that is behind his success, in easier seasons and challenging times.

Along with the challenges of Covid, Mike has dealt with other difficulties. As beautiful as the inn's location is, off the beautiful and iconic Highway 1 along the rugged California coast, the site creates its own challenges when the road washes out during the heavy rains of winter. During a recent particularly heavy winter, the road was washed out both from the south and the north of the property. This isolation could have closed Mike's business, but his passion and creativity allowed him to come up with the idea of helicoptering his guests in while the road was feverishly being reopened. The creativity of the solution also gave his guests the unique adventure of seeing the beautiful coast from the air. Passion was contagious for both owner and client.

This is the power of passion: You engage at a level of higher quality that sets you apart from your competition, and you find more success at the same time. Whatever the industry, this principle holds true. You can conduct your sales effort in a surface-level manner, clocking in and doing only what is required. Or, when you feel real passion for your work, you can find creative ways to make the experience richer for you and your clients. You'll want to understand your product more. You'll be more enthusiastic, which will help you convince others of its value. Then you'll find more thrill in developing your business relationships.

I want to talk to someone who has a real passion for what they are pursuing in their life. I want that person on my team. Your passion for your work can be exponentially increased when your dedication is expanded by working with others. The whole idea of teamwork is not a cliché—it's a positive for the development of relationships and your business. The strength of others will help you gain the confidence and support you need as you build and grow, and your passion will draw others to you.

A recent Gallup poll focused on the mental wellness of workers in the Covid era of remote working. It found that fewer than one-third of people felt engaged with their work, and they were less connected with the broader purpose of where they worked.[2] This drop in engagement started with the pandemic, but it does not appear to be getting better. Younger workers, Millennials, and Gen Xers all felt they were less cared for and less heard at work.[3] Understandably, it can be concluded that they feel less passion for what they are doing on a daily basis. With the growth in remote working, workers likely develop less and less attachment to their places of work. It's much harder to develop deep friendships when you are not working with people in a shared space.

When I was working at Goldman, I saw my colleagues every day. In addition to knowing about each other's lives, I knew what my colleagues were working on, and they knew my projects. We had a sense of common purpose that helped fuel our passion. When we work at home, there are no "chance" happenings in the hallway or around the proverbial water cooler or the kombucha machine. We are often more focused or siloed on our individual projects.

A recent Glassdoor poll found that fewer and fewer

Passion

workers had a best friend at work.[4] A conference call just does not connect in the same way that people do when sitting around the same table, discussing their work and their common goal. Opportunities to be empathetic; to listen; to develop a passion for your work, individual projects, and the work and projects of your colleagues and the company as a whole are fewer. That said, remote work and a reliance on digital communication are the new reality for a number of people. This makes it even more important to clarify your passion for your job and find ways to keep that passion fire burning as much as it was on your first day. I would also argue that increasing the face time among you and your team as much as possible is essential.

There is much cynicism about face time within an organization, but it has real value. You get a clearer understanding of the goals of the company. It also shows a level of caring and interest on the part of employees and employers. Leaders of an organization are better when they are seen. A leader walking the floor of any organization is a physical representation of passion and caring for enterprise and employees. All of this underscores the importance of the topics we have discussed and will discuss in this book. The idea of developing an empathetic approach is better practiced and developed when you are meeting in person and not digitally. Companies can sell their purpose more convincingly when there is real face-to-face communication. Your skills of empathy and listening grow—and are displayed at their best—when practiced in real time with others. In-person interaction feels better and helps us grow

CONNECTABILITY

our passion, and being together (or at the very least, in a video call) helps us show our passion.

In this current climate, we need to nourish our passion more than ever. And whenever you can, meet a client or potential client in person. Bring your passion for your work to develop a relationship with them, and let the client see it in your eyes. Passion opens windows for all of us, just as it has for my daughter in her pursuit of a very different business than financial services.

My daughter Emily is building a career in theater arts, and she is passionate about her pursuits personally and professionally. While attending Wesleyan University she discovered a love of theater arts and shifted her entire trajectory. After graduating Phi Beta Kappa from Wesleyan with a degree in theater arts, she then received a master's at the London Academy of Music and Dramatic Art. From there, Emily had many choices of potential careers that might have had an easier path or more immediate monetary results. But she remained dedicated to the craft of visual art through acting, writing, and directing, which can be quite daunting. You are judged in every way possible through the critical eyes and ears of audience and critics. Yet Emily has devoted herself to it, and this dedication has brought her short films to the attention of international film festivals. This level of quality cannot be accomplished solely through time directed to the project of writing, acting, and directing. It can only be accomplished through continual dedication and passion.

Emily is now living in London, pursuing many branches

Passion

of this passion. Her road is a difficult one, as 80 percent of films fail to be commercially successful or make money at all. However, her vision is driven by passion, and that is the invisible commodity that will allow her to succeed.

Developing relationships and sales is challenging under the best of circumstances. Having a passion for your work and the process is not only rewarding but also gives you an advantage over your competitors. Often your competition is only going through the motions. In a world as challenging as the one we live in, slipping by with minimal enthusiasm will not be enough to succeed. Passion will help drive your desire to connect, to develop, to reach higher.

Passion keeps us dedicated, focused, and in the game, all of which help us develop the other skills we have discussed. People who are truly passionate are often more empathetic, as their passion drives them to understand more and discover more about the people they are interacting with.

Passion will also give us the confidence to take more risks. We are most accustomed to thinking of monetary risk, and that's important and valid; no one likes to lose funds and material resources while building one's business. But I would say an even more challenging risk is personal—risking one's confidence and personal capital. These risks can feel even more uncomfortable at times. Yet success isn't possible without taking the leap, and so we have to lean in and do the hard thing anyway.

To build successful relationships, we have to become more comfortable with risk. Which is why we'll explore this essential principle next.

CHAPTER 4

Risk

When we hear the word risk, we generally think of physical or financial risk. As an example, working with horses brings with it a certain physical risk. You can immediately picture falling off a horse or being kicked by one. The stock market brings risk too. Investing in a single stock brings potential financial risk, which comes from having a portfolio that is not balanced. Yet I would say the most intimidating risk is personal, when we risk our reputation or public perception.

I didn't grow up with horses but always felt a kinship with these majestic and powerful animals, along with a desire to train and compete with them. When I started working with them, it didn't feel that risky, either from my naivete or an

CONNECTABILITY

overconfidence that all would be well. But I still knew there was an element of risk. Yet I wanted this dream enough to take the risk. So I learned. I trained. When I purchased a horse ranch in California, my trainer, JT, and I developed a credible program and achieved a measure of success in the cutting horse world.

This success was largely achieved through the talent of one particular horse, a stunning chestnut stallion with an incredible physical confirmation (the structure and shape of his body) and equally impressive bloodlines. He also represented a higher risk factor, not so much because of the degree of difficulty in training him but because of the expectation of success he brought with him. His name was Rocket, and he was a known commodity in the tight-knit world of cutting horses.

Hick Chicaroo (aka Rocket) was sired by Doc's Hickory (1973) out of Roosters Chicaroo (1996). In the cutting horse world, Rocket was a well-bred stallion. He was magnificent and true to his name. He was a powerful athlete. Unfortunately, Mr. Webster fails me when describing the feeling of elation and joy I felt working with this magnificent animal. When sitting astride Rocket, I was balanced on twelve hundred pounds of pure muscle, fierce attitude, and determined resolve. It was exhilarating—as if I had parked my Toyota and jumped into a Ferrari. All this power and ability came with a high-risk component. Like anything finely grafted and technically skilled, there is not much margin for error and a high degree of risk—not only risk of injury but also risk of failure. I might look good on the

Risk

track in a Ferrari, but there is a higher level of risk compared to driving my Toyota to the grocery store.

Risk comes in different packages and profiles. The important part is that all success comes with risk, and it must be adopted in various ways.

Over months of practice together, we achieved a level of understanding: We shared a mutual desire to achieve. Rocket was competitive, like me, and his heart was all in when it came to achieving the desired outcome. In our own way, we were willing to accept the risk to achieve success. In the sport of cutting, you have two and a half minutes to demonstrate that, as a team, you can control at least two cows in front of a herd of other cows. The arena feels electric, and the horse can feel it just as well as the rider. Rocket knew he was on the field of play, and he wanted to prove he was the best. We both did, and so we would both be in a high-adrenaline state, which heightened the risk factor within the experience. The natural increase in adrenaline levels increases your risk as you push the envelope to take on more challenging cows to prove your abilities. As we became used to working together, though, the level of felt risk began to dissipate, leaving the high of competition and the joy in what we were accomplishing. Ultimately, we achieved a good deal of success in the show pen. Desire can be an incredible motivator to accept a risk and do so willingly. It's valuable fuel that helps us step forward into discomfort. Another tool that helps us step into risk is practice.

What we do over and over again comes to feel more

CONNECTABILITY

comfortable. As in any sport, the number of repetitions helps us to understand risk, become comfortable with it, and achieve success.

As a salesperson, I had to get comfortable with the discomfort of taking risks. For me, making cold calls felt risky, a risk I would have preferred to avoid, but early in my career, I had to make them. With each call, you're taking a risk that often feels deeply personal—of getting rejected—whatever the context, and you're risking failure. But to be successful at anything, you must be comfortable with taking a risk, or if you are uncomfortable, you must be willing to do it anyway. My desire to be successful despite my fear of failure gave me the push I needed to take risks.

When I joined Goldman, I had a reputation as a solid salesperson in the bond market. Yet not coming up through the customary top-twenty-MBA-program route like most of my other Goldman colleagues, I felt a real potential risk of failure. I could only go down from there. Of course, that was not my intent. My developed relationships came through with immediate business, which impressed my new employer. Nevertheless, there was further need to succeed. I strongly desired to reestablish and prove myself at this very prestigious firm.

One afternoon, a salesman from another division approached me to ask if I would consider covering an account of his, the Kamehameha Schools Bishop Estate. The Bishop Estate was not going to be a buyer of equity positions, and the salesman felt he did not have the time or expertise to cover a fixed-income-only account.

Risk

At this time, most financial services firms divided account coverage into equities and fixed income (bonds). Today that is not always the case, as low interest rates have driven most firms to combine bonds and equities into one sales coverage division. But this was the day of high interest rates, and bonds were the dominant market, like Tom Wolfe wrote about in his novel *The Bonfire of the Vanities*.

I agreed to take coverage of the account, and the manager of the office agreed but with one stipulation: I could not visit the account, which was based in Hawaii. For any client development on the beaches of Waikiki, he would first require the account to be doing consistent business with the firm—which it was not at the time of this reassignment.

In a later chapter, I'll discuss this account in further detail, as it would eventually become the most important client of my career. At this juncture, I wish to explore the element of risk involved in accepting this reassignment. The client might not have wanted a change in coverage; they might not have ever developed into a significant account for the firm and thus could have become a drag on my career. However, I was interested in this organization and the Hawaiian culture, which drove me to take the career risk to cover this seemingly small account. It was a risk worth taking.

In either building a relationship or selling a product, there are no truly safe passageways. You will have to engage in risk-taking. No one likes to be rejected, in work or personal life. Think about asking someone for that first date. Your risk is in the possibility of the person rejecting your

CONNECTABILITY

invitation. Think of those cold calls. The people you are calling might say no. Rejection does not feel good in any arena—but how can you possibly get a yes without asking?

People can be so risk-averse that even within the safety of an already established relationship, they may decline to extend themselves. I often get coffee in the morning, and for me, the coffee is just the supporting act. The most intriguing event on center stage is getting to observe and interact with people at the start of the day, when they're oftentimes more willing to be vulnerable.

One day I sat next to a couple I could only assume had been together for years. The man was observing another couple sitting across the room and commented how much the man across the café adored his wife, observing how he and she were riveted on each other as if they had just met. (I personally preferred to believe they were instead wrapped in the glow of a well-tended intimate relationship they'd been enjoying for years.) The wife of the man doing the observing commented that she wished her husband looked at her in that same manner. He replied, perhaps being defensive or maybe just stating what he felt was fact, "I look at you that way all the time! I think you just don't see me."

It was a sad interaction that felt like a missed opportunity for real connection. From my vantage point, the man appeared to be commenting on the other man's adoration in order to tell his wife how he felt about her—his way of permitting himself to reveal his emotions, indirectly, at a safer distance. She, not recognizing what he was doing, criticized him because she just wanted to hear it directly!

Risk

For whatever reason, it felt like too much risk for the husband to tell his wife how he felt in a clear, intimate manner.

Risk also exists within the confines of our established business relationships—in developing unique solutions to problems, thinking beyond the norm, and being willing to expose ourselves. Staying within a confined set of rules or beliefs is not necessarily the best way to demonstrate that you can bring value to your clients. Taking a different approach is riskier, but it can bring you the best solutions. It also demonstrates to your client you are interested in their needs by listening in a thoughtful, empathetic manner. As a relationship progresses and grows, you will also encounter new risks.

Relationship building has a trajectory and a rhythm as trust develops. With both personal and business relationships, the beginnings are usually more formal affairs. The necessary introductory phase is all about the details of practical information and getting to know each other in small ways. You will most likely present yourself in the best possible way. However, as you develop a closer relationship with the other person, there is a growing ease with each other. (At least, this is what we hope for.) This means as we grow closer, we offer each other more ways to have problems with each other. We learn more about the other, ways we're different, ways we may annoy each other. And now we have more unforced errors on both sides. But it's essential we take this risk to get closer; without it, we're just left living and working on the surface.

As these differences are inevitably revealed in the process

of building a relationship, we don't need to see it as a death knell. Rather, we can see it as something that will help define its boundaries. In setting boundaries, you will be able to mitigate the risk while still opening into it, and thus secure better returns overall. We cannot all be the same. And why would we want to be? Understanding how our differences can translate into a better relationship will keep the trust and development intact and growing.

Risk comes in many different packages, and taking risks yields a variety of wonderful outcomes. Mike Freed, whom I mentioned in the previous chapter, undertook a level of risk to get where he is with the Post Ranch Inn.

The beautiful area of Big Sur was originally inhabited by Costanoan Indians, until they succumbed to disease introduced by soldiers and missionaries. After this tragedy, the land around Big Sur was virtually uninhabited until 1848, when William Post homesteaded one hundred sixty acres. Over time, the Post family acquired about fifteen hundred acres total, which includes the modern-day Post Ranch Inn. Mike Freed originally worked as a successful real estate attorney who frequented the Monterey peninsula, especially Big Sur, and over the years befriended Billy Post, a descendant of William Post. Mike offered his services as a real estate attorney.

Eventually these two men together developed what is now considered the number one small inn in the United States. This partnership involved risk for both men, as well as desire that led them to take the risk. They both wanted to acknowledge the contribution of the original Indian inhabitants

Risk

and protect the land. Passion played a big role here too, as Mike had a great love of the outdoors. Changing careers was a risky move for Mike, as he had a successful career in law and real estate development. Creating a hotel on their family legacy was a risk for the Post family too. At that time, Big Sur was not on anybody's list of places to visit. However, this partnership understood the probabilities of a successful collaboration. Through their vision and hard work, they created an amazing project that after completion and years of successful operation appears riskless. We should judge risk not after it has been successfully taken but in the beginning, when all the variables are uncomfortable and probability is being assessed. It's easy to look at this fabulous property and assume it was always like it is today. But it wasn't. This achievement required passion and risk.

The famous restaurateur Danny Meyer is another person who took a risk to build a business based on relationships. I met Danny when he was a manager and working "the front of the house"—in other words, the roles most visible to the customer (i.e., busboy, bartender, host, server, maître d', and manager). At the age of twenty-seven and with little money, he opened his first restaurant in an area of New York that wasn't noted for restaurant excellence. Restaurants even in the most fashionable areas frequently fail, but Danny successfully managed to create a unique restaurant experience. He believed in his passion, and in many ways he changed the restaurant business from a more formal, standoffish, fine-dining event to an experience that was interested in the patron. His waitstaff was knowledgeable and welcoming.

CONNECTABILITY

Computer data helped him remember names of patrons and when they last visited, in addition to other personal details. He combined tools like this with the analog warmth of personal communication.

I have many stories about people in the hospitality business who have taken on risk to pursue their passion, but we also see this narrative in other ventures. Billy Shore was the chief of staff for a Democratic politician who was once the odds-on favorite to be the next presidential candidate for the Democratic Party. Yet in an incredible twist of fate, this politician fell from grace due to an extramarital affair. It would have been easier for Billy Shore to have retreated to another job in the political arena; however, when this door closed, he chose to take a tremendous risk and embrace his passion for philanthropic pursuits. With his sister, he established Share Our Strength, a philanthropic organization that grew to be a $60 million effort. As there are sixteen million children who go hungry in the US every day, their first campaign was to eliminate childhood hunger. They established the No Kid Hungry campaign. This pursuit was much more complicated than getting another position in the political sphere. The success of Share Our Strength is due to his willingness to take on risk.

Risk-taking does not always involve putting money on the line. Anytime you put yourself in a vulnerable position that has the potential for great reward, you are taking a risk. The reward cannot come without the risk. Personal risk and business risk still make you vulnerable—taking these risks requires a level of confidence and belief in yourself. Even

Risk

if you don't currently have the talent or tools you need to realize a goal, you understand you have the ability to learn and achieve. Even failure will be a learning experience that will mitigate the risk of your next project.

Taking risks is about embracing the real possibilities in front of you, and whether you're building a hotel, creating a restaurant, starting a philanthropic endeavor, or developing accounts and building those relationships, these tasks can be done with a high probability of success.

Understand that nothing is 100 percent risk-free. But we can do our best to understand or quantify the percentages assigned to outcomes with probability risk-taking. This style of risk-taking is well-thought-out and gives us the opportunity of moving into the unknown with the highest likelihood of success. While the probabilities we assign are bound to be imperfect, the exercise is a good way to think about possible outcomes and refine the risk you are willing to take.

Much of the conversation and language around risk is framed in the negative—shielding oneself from financial risk, insuring oneself against risk, hedging risk—but I suggest we also understand risk as a positive—a framework, if you will, for achieving success. For this, it can help to understand that we take risks in our everyday life. Think of all those moments throughout each day, large and small, in your work and personal worlds, when you become vulnerable and extend yourself in some way. Every time you pick up the phone to make an outgoing phone call, you are risking your personal capital. We don't know what someone will say, and for most of us, that's stepping out of our comfort zone.

CONNECTABILITY

The negative aspects of risk are mitigated by the amount of preparation we put into achieving our goals. We can also see risk as the positive affirmation that we are preparing ourselves for great things to happen. Risk, vulnerability, and uncertainty are generally viewed in a negative light, yet, by embracing these elements, we demonstrate a willingness to be closer and to invest in the relationships we are building. Viewing these risks in a probability framework will help us become more comfortable with using risk and vulnerability to achieve.

As I look back on my introduction to the Kamehameha Schools Bishop Estate account, the risk in taking it on felt larger then than how I see it now. In fairness, though, to my younger self as the new guy on the desk, it was important for me to produce with accounts that were more traditional and had a regular flow of business in the dynamic, fixed-income market at that time. So, accepting and devoting time and effort to develop an account that did not appear to be traditional was risky. I did it because I knew some risk-taking was going to be necessary to succeed. I also had a deep interest in both the needs of the unique Hawaiian culture and in the account's goal: to create a school through the will of the last remaining relative of King Kamehameha I, who had unified the Hawaiian Islands. To help this unique educational institution meet their needs, I was driven to take further risks in thinking creatively and outside the box to come up with innovative and unusual solutions.

Fueled by this interest, I was diligent in following up on the account's many requests. The estate was located

Risk

many time zones from New York, but I stayed close to the account and established consistent communication, which enhanced my opportunities for success. This is always good to remember when attempting to mitigate risk. The best—and least risky—place to be is close to the account.

The same concept applies to horses. Many people have a fear of horses, and it's no wonder, as they're tremendously large, strong, and sensitive animals who will physically protect themselves when they feel fear. What's interesting, though, is we tend to protect ourselves by standing a distance away from them. But the problem with that approach is you then give the horse the opportunity to extend their legs if they want to kick—meaning you are at the business end of their legs. However, if you stand close to the horse, they cannot extend their legs, making this the best and least risky place to be when working with them. Staying close not only helps mitigate risk but also gives you the opportunity to better use empathetic skill, listen, and learn—allowing you to be more creative and knowledgeable in your approach.

Creativity and knowledge together are another foundational element in relationship-building success. Let's zoom in closer on these next.

CHAPTER 5

Creativity and Knowledge

Creativity is an all-important pillar of relationship building. It enables innovative solutions to problem-solving and distinguishes you as a unique, solutions-driven collaborator. Knowledge is another crucial component and a necessary building block. When combined, these elements serve as a catalyst to forming strong, solutions-based relationships.

I certainly experienced this in my own career. As I built my relationship with the Kamehameha Schools, I learned more about how they operated and the unique problems they faced. The Kamehameha Schools Bishop Estate was created through the will of Princess Pauahi Bishop, and the sole beneficiary was the Kamehameha Schools, a K–12 school system dedicated to the children of Hawaiian descent. The other principal business of the estate was the management of their vast real estate holdings. With careful listening, I was able to discern what their greatest needs were rather than simply selling them securities. As I became more knowledgeable, I was able to become more creative, too, as I thought through potential solutions.

Like other institutions in seasonal industries, the Kamehameha Schools had certain revenue shortfalls throughout the school year—generally around the time when tuitions were not being paid. Using bank loans to cover these shortfalls was putting an undue burden on the school administration and was costly compared to prevailing market rates. So I started thinking about alternatives they might consider for financing the everyday operation of their institution.

At the time, educational institutions in the US were generally approaching their finances traditionally. Still, a small handful were trying new ideas, such as using the commercial paper market blended with other forms of institutional borrowing. It represented a useful way to bridge periods of low revenue. I felt commercial paper could be a valuable tool in the management of the Kamehameha Schools' finances.

Commercial paper is one of the oldest forms of unsecured short-term debt, a form of unsecured public borrowing

Creativity and Knowledge

that is well over one hundred years old. It's typically used for financing payroll, accounts payable, and inventories and meeting other short-term liabilities.[1] Usually sold at a discount from face value, commercial paper reflects prevailing market interest rates. Think of it as a loan to finance short-term obligations as a bridge until more permanent financing or revenue comes into an entity. Maturities range from a few days to 270 days. This financing method is convenient because it allows issuers to avoid the hurdles and expense of applying for and securing continuous business loans. Unlike with many other forms of public borrowing, issuers don't need Securities and Exchange Commission (SEC) registration.

Goldman is one of the principle dealers in the commercial paper market. For the most part, their issuers were industrial corporations or financial institutions rather than educational institutions. However, as I considered myself a creative thinker, I approached our investment bankers to see if the firm would consider proposing the use of commercial paper to the Bishop Estate.

The Bishop Estate owns roughly one-eighth of the State of Hawaii. The estate's financial condition was incredibly solid, and I assumed they would be creditworthy, although the situation would still be a little unusual because of their tax status as an educational entity.

After review, I received the green light to approach them to see if they would consider using this unique form of short-term borrowing. I don't think anyone had ever approached the estate with any creative financing ideas,

CONNECTABILITY

as they assumed there was no need or the management wouldn't be interested. This wasn't the case: The board of trustees was interested in this idea, which would simplify their borrowing process and lower their borrowing costs.

I arranged the meeting with our bankers and the estate's chief financial officer, and we began the process of developing a commercial paper program for them. This was not difficult but took time, as the most important part was getting the rating agencies to become comfortable with the Bishop Estate as a public borrower in order for them to obtain a high rating. (Commercial paper, similar to other forms of public borrowing, required a rating by a third party to attest to their creditworthiness. Standard and Poor's and Moody's are the two most prominent credit rating organizations.) Both of these goals were accomplished, and thus the Bishop Estate established a substantial commercial borrowing program. The estate was not an obvious user of this financing tool, but with creative thinking I was able to help them establish a valuable program, which added sophistication to their operation and established substantial cost savings.

You have greater opportunities for success when you're both knowledgeable and creative. The two go hand in hand. There is no substitute for knowledge, and that knowledge opens the creative door. The more you know about your organization and the people of the institutions you are developing a relationship with, the more value you can bring to problem-solving. Knowledge is not a stagnant commodity. The key is being open to learning more as you

Creativity and Knowledge

develop your relationships. "If it ain't broke, don't fix it" is a sure way to become irrelevant, fast.

ExxonMobil is an example of a company losing value either because of a lack of creativity or because their main line of business becomes stagnant. It was added to the Dow Jones Industrial Average in 1928 and removed in August of 2020. At one point it was the largest company in the world, with a stock price of $500 per share and a market capitalization of $446 billion. It is still worth $446 billion, but its stock price is $118 per share, while the world's largest company, Apple, has a market cap of $2.93 trillion. Now clearly, Exxon is still a valuable company, but its failure to make itself more relevant with the continued advancement of knowledge surrounding oil, the environment, and climate change has been a factor in its falling fortunes. In the same way, you must continually keep your knowledge current so you can remain valuable over time to your clients and relationships.

I once worked with a woman who specialized in mortgage securities, which at the time were the most complicated element in the fixed-income market. She was incredibly successful not only because of her basic intelligence but also her ongoing relevance due to her "at the moment" knowledge of this complicated market. She never rested on her knowledge from yesterday. She was always up to the minute and her clients were aware of this, appreciating that quality. She was passionate about the markets in general, and that passion drove her desire to increase her knowledge.

CONNECTABILITY

Passion leads to more creativity. If you're passionate about your work, you will find more ways to develop and promote creative solutions.

I've often thought of doctors going through years of training, years of working in hospitals, and then coming out and establishing their practice, where they must continue adding to all that previous learning—because medicine is constantly changing. No one wants a doctor who is stuck in the past. I would certainly prefer the doctor who is up-to-date on the latest in medical advancements.

All aspects of our rapidly changing world rely on possessing up-to-date knowledge. Your relationship building is a dynamic event and requires you to not only stay current on your clients but to also stay current on changes in the marketplace. Simply put, the world is not a stagnant place. It is dynamic, and staying knowledgeable keeps you ahead of the game and allows a more creative thought process. Staying informed and insightful will keep you relevant and valuable to your clients.

We tend to think about being creative in an artistic way—as a painter or a musician. Yet creativity is a far broader concept, as it is a key component in all walks of life. When you are developing relationships, being creative means thinking and advancing unique solutions; being willing to take the risk to do things differently; understanding that we exist in a dynamic environment and clearly not all solutions fit all clients. Because there is no one solution, we need creativity to identify and bring in more options. Your solutions can and should become as dynamic and will drive your success.

Creativity and Knowledge

Creativity will make you more valuable to your clients and to the relationships you are building.

We tend to pay lip service to the ability to think outside the box, but the reality is most of us get stuck in the methodology of what works—until it doesn't work. The Covid crisis prompted many businesses to reexamine their methodology and create a model that not only met the real challenge of the moment, but could also be more successful than their previous model.

One such business is Handlebar, a coffee bar started by a couple who had been very successful bicycle racing in Europe. Initially, Handlebar occupied a small space in downtown Santa Barbara. Owners Kim and Aaron roasted and served coffee and espresso drinks with a limited amount of high-quality baked goods on the side. Their product was very much in the European tradition, with a "proper" cappuccino—no venti pumpkin spice lattes here. Serving a quality product behind a massive espresso machine, their business grew, and after a while they established a new, larger location in an area with limited parking. Because of the quality of their product, though, people found a way to park and happily stood in line. Handlebar had a fairly typical model for a high-quality, specialized coffee bar.

Then came the Covid crisis and they were forced to shut down. This is where the owners became creative and pivoted their business to a new model that allowed them to keep the business running, with a greater diversity of products and limited overhead.

CONNECTABILITY

When allowed to reopen, they immediately adhered to the county health requirements: They closed their kitchen, removed the tables, and established signage for social distancing. They were able to keep their employees by limiting their hours. People don't drink a lot of coffee at four in the afternoon; the majority of revenue occurs between seven a.m. and one p.m. To supplement the lost revenue, they began offering reasonably priced, restaurant-quality bulk food products such as flours, olive oil, and sugar. It turned out a lot of their clients were suddenly baking more often and happy to purchase some of the staples while they picked up their coffee at Handlebar. Additionally, the business started to stock wine from local wineries. Instead of the usual high percentage markup that is common to wine retail, Handlebar marked up less, giving their customers a bargain price while giving the winemaker an additional outlet.

Dropping a large percent of revenue was not something they had considered in their original business plan. However, adding different revenue channels to their high-quality coffee product resulted in a revenue model that showed year-over-year increases. As an additional benefit, the owners and employees were able to go home early to be with family and friends and to think about the next new product channel or way to provide service and value. Maybe they even took a bike ride like the old days.

Bell's is another example of a business that made an immediate pivot in business model. Taking advantage of the PPP loan program, they were able to retain their entire staff during Covid. They remodeled their interior dining to

Creativity and Knowledge

adhere to the distancing rules, and more importantly, they created a delightful outdoor patio space. Another critical change was the type of dining offered, moving to offer a five-course prix-fixe menu with a standard service charge and with seating available by reservation only. They started with dinner service five nights a week and eventually added lunch, while remaining closed Tuesday and Wednesday. These modest but critical business model changes resulted in better control of their inventory and service, while allowing them to retain their employees and still provide an exemplary hospitality experience. Dinner at Bell's is truly memorable. Oh, and did I mention that this is a more profitable model, allowing their business to grow?

The alterations these two businesses made to their models appear on the surface to be minor and not that creative. But I would disagree with that assessment. Creative changes in one's business model or one's life model are often nuanced. Often the biggest challenge is the desire to creatively adjust at all. That's because change of any kind is difficult. It is so much easier to remain the same, comfortable in what we know. With both Handlebar and Bell's, some of this change was forced, but that's true of life. Much of what prompts our creativity are those things we did not plan for. It's also true that the larger the business, the more difficult being nimble and creative can be. Like a ship in the ocean, changing course takes time; however, that does not mean it is impossible. But additional time and planning are required.

Creativity can make all the difference. And while there's no substitute for knowledge, sometimes creativity can also

CONNECTABILITY

bail out an occasional lack of knowledge. No matter how much time and energy you put into obtaining knowledge and staying current in your field, you cannot know it all.

This was my experience when I was given a new role in the Goldman San Francisco office. I had developed a successful career fueled by knowledge of the fixed-income market and the development of meaningful relationships with my accounts. My boss and mentor's career was also on an upward trajectory, as he was chosen to head up the division in London. Within a few days of the announcement that he was being transferred, I was put in charge of the San Francisco office. There was no warm-up for this job. One day my boss was there and ready to solve problems, and the next day he was gone and the problem-solving fell to me. I didn't have the chance to develop this skill set before taking charge, but luckily, I still could tap into creativity.

On the afternoon of my first day in this new role, my longtime partner came to me and said, "We have a problem."

Now that is never a good start to a day, and this time was no exception. It turned out our largest account was reneging on a trade. In an over-the-counter market where literally hundreds of millions of dollars are traded on your verbal confirmation, reneging on a commitment like that was a very big problem.

As it turned out, this was not an ordinary trade, either, but a complicated mortgage private placement. Mortgage-backed securities were already difficult and complex, and this one had an extra level of complexity since it was privately placed and had a few other covenants that made it

Creativity and Knowledge

quite unique. Thinking I could reason with the account and get them to accept the trade, I called the portfolio manager. What transpired was anything but pleasant. The account client called me and my firm a number of unattractive adjectives as he also accused me of not knowing anything about this security—while he knew everything. He was not going to accept the trade.

Knowledge is truly a key ingredient to success, but a crucial piece is knowing what you don't know. This is where creativity comes into play, especially when it can be enhanced with empathy and listening. My pathway through this difficulty was to first admit that he was correct: I did not have an intimate knowledge of this particular security. However, I did have the foresight to start asking reasonably intelligent questions, which began to fill in some gaps. I also knew a lot about this particular individual, including the fact that he had great respect for my boss, the head of the division, who was legendary in the fixed-income market and especially in the mortgage-backed securities market.

I told the client that the partner in charge of the division had been intimately involved with the creation of this private placement, and he had thought it would be a perfect fit. I then asked if he would allow me to set up a call with him to have a brief discussion before he rejected the trade. This was agreed to, and I immediately arranged the conference call. As it turned out, my boss knew more than the client, so that was a knowledge-based "leg up." In the end, the client accepted the trade.

What did I learn from this unfortunate event? Having

CONNECTABILITY

knowledge is important and makes you able to navigate the difficult questions and have appropriate answers. But it is equally important to recognize your gaps in knowledge and deal with those creatively. Like I mentioned earlier, it's exactly what our teachers always tell us in school: There are no dumb questions. And when they say their door is always open, they mean it. They want us to show up and ask. You have to be willing to take a risk (admit that you did not know something) and do it—ask the questions.

Asking questions to fill in our knowledge gaps does two things. First, it shows you are interested and perhaps even have passion for the subject at hand. Second, it shows you are listening. This works just as well when there's a problem to be solved as when there's a test on the horizon. If I ask questions, the client knows I care and I am listening. The combination of listening and asking questions is an effective tool when building relationships and helps to understand the problem at hand. The perception that asking questions indicates a problematic lack of knowledge is false; in reality, the practice helps establish interest and showcases your desire to build a deeper creative platform.

I've always felt problems were a positive when it came to developing client relationships. If everything is going well, what is left to solve for them? Problems, and gaps in knowledge, allow you the perfect platform to demonstrate your empathetic nature. They give you space to listen, inquire, learn, and be creative—which may not only solve a difficult problem but also create unexpected rewards.

While I didn't love starting out my day hearing the

Creativity and Knowledge

phrase "we have a problem," the issue led to multiple positive outcomes. I showed respect to the client. I owned up to what I knew and what I didn't know. Then I showed him I was able to think creatively and find a solution.

This included connecting him with an important person—the head of our division. People who feel they're important like talking to important people. I showed the client I had access to important people and respected him enough to connect them. You have a better chance of solving a problem when you can level the playing field. Taking your ego out of the equation opens up a whole world of better connectivity. If we make it all about ourselves, there is no room for growth into a truly functioning relationship.

From my boss's standpoint, he knew he had a manager who wasn't going to fail when there was a real problem. He knew I was going to think creatively and find a solution, and my ego wasn't going to get in the way. Not only did the trade go forward but so did the client relationship.

Over my career—and especially when I stepped into managing the Goldman San Francisco office—I learned that information is always changing. Whatever your educational background, you've got to devote a significant amount of time to staying knowledgeable and relevant. I know when I finished school, I was hopeful I would never have to take another test again. But what I discovered was the tests never stopped; they were just presented in a different form. We are tested continually as our relationships change and our business changes. Preparing for that test is less obvious than when there was specific coursework to study.

CONNECTABILITY

If I hadn't navigated this problem with a certain level of knowledge (and admitting lack of knowledge) and creativity, the outcome would have been worse, and it would have then been a challenge for others in the office to see me as a problem solver. Doing what I needed to do to develop knowledge while tapping into my creativity saved me.

One aspect of creativity is working with what's available to you in the present moment. Which brings us to the next chapter on being present and available.

CHAPTER 6

Present and Available

The other day, I was driving home after an early dinner at one of my favorite Marin County restaurants. I was gliding along and noticed how oddly relaxing it was to drive the speed limit: You're not furtively checking the mirror for flashing lights demanding you pull over. You're not competing for position with other cars also driving too fast. You are just driving along in your lane as if you own the road and have no particular place to be.

When the light turned yellow, I comfortably came to a stop at the light, which changed to red as I waited. I was the first car in the intersection, and thus the red sphere was directly in front of me. I was mesmerized by the light and saw nothing else around it.

I suddenly felt so relaxed. It was as if the red light had told me that I could take a time-out from everything around it—the disappointments, the tasks I had to do, the lack of achievement I was feeling on that particular day. The light invited me to sit there without worry or concern about my destination. For sixty to ninety seconds, I was conscious of this amazing relief. Then the light turned green and the rest of life rushed back. But for that short window, I was truly present and available to the moment and what was right in front of me.

This was a moment of understanding what extreme focus and being present without distraction would feel like. I don't always do this, but more and more, I try. When I do, amazing experiences flood in. Textures and feelings become richer. Projects become more fun; even the moment or task at hand seems pretty simple. Being present is not an easy task, as we live in a world of distractions.

"I am really busy!" We hear this refrain all the time, and somehow it's become a catchall phrase and excuse to release us from all sorts of failures in relationship building. When we feel we're so busy, we try to multitask and are even less likely to be fully present in what we're experiencing.

These distractions, whether in our mind or the physical world around us, weaken our availability to focus on the project in front of us. When building relationships, these distractions hurt our ability to build in a deep manner. If

Present and Available

we want to understand our client, we must bring our full focus and attention. Our ability to be present is what drives the richness of our relationships and life.

So how does that fit in this book? Well, while passion can make a massive difference in how you connect and do your work, so can finding ways to open to all that meets you in the details. We can take pleasure in little things, and not only will the large portion of our life devoted to working feel more enjoyable, but we'll also find treasures we'd never notice if we blew right by them. Being present and available to the moment, whether with people we connect with or situations that surround us, is a game changer leading to more enjoyment and opportunity.

Most of us need this shift, desperately. Gallup, in its *State of the Global Workplace: 2022 Report*, found that along with dissatisfaction, workers are experiencing staggering rates of both disengagement and unhappiness. Sixty percent of people reported being emotionally detached at work and 19 percent as being miserable. Only 33 percent reported feeling engaged—and that is even lower than in 2020.[1]

This is a sad state of affairs, because most of us spend a large portion of our lives working. Beyond opening to the opportunities for pleasure we can find in the moment, we have to be able to find some passion for our work too. If we've done that, I believe there's plenty of room to drill down and find ways to maximize enjoyment and opportunity in our daily moments, many of which aren't always exciting. Focusing on the present moment and being available for what that moment has to offer is a discipline that opens the door to stronger, more rewarding business success.

I found this to be true in my own career in financial services, which I discovered quite by accident (and fortunate circumstance). After I had graduated from the University of California at Santa Barbara, and between undergraduate and graduate school, I was working as a pool maintenance man for Santa Monica City College, reporting to the head of Parks and Recreation. The Parks director had taken an interest in me, as I was about to head for business school. He recommended I qualify as a beach lifeguard, as it was a better paying job, more varied, and more interesting. I followed his advice, and it was exactly as he had portended. Lifeguarding was easily enjoyable, I was making double the pay, and the hours aligned with my school schedule.

Soon after I embarked on this path, my father, a brilliant attorney, asked me to meet him at his office for lunch. I suspected this would be a lecture on my life pursuits, and indeed, it was. As I was about to be married and going to grad school, he suggested that a job with more future would be in order. And—for better or worse—I listened to his advice. Months later during business school, I took a job at a bank as a loan officer trainee. It wasn't my favorite job—especially compared to my work at the beach, which I naturally took easy enjoyment in.

However, I was fortunate to have a training officer interested in my job satisfaction. He turned out to be a critical part of my journey to finding a job I could have passion for.

Present and Available

My supervisor in the loan officer program understood I didn't like the job and was considering returning to being a lifeguard while going to business school. He then suggested I interview with some other departments within the bank—as he explained, the bank offered many services besides lending money. After several false starts, I transferred to the investment department of the bank, where I was exposed to the securities markets. As it turned out, this was a stroke of good luck since I loved this work. As I've mentioned, this job granted exposure to literally everything that was occurring in the world. I was able to have a credible conversation on virtually any current event. Information in the markets flows all day and all night.

As much passion as I had for my job, not every task was exciting. Although learning and discovering the intricacies of the securities markets held a constant fascination for me, the day-to-day details did not always involve executing multimillion-dollar trades. Similar to many positions, there's plenty of boring stuff to go around. Yet when you're truly present and available—to people and the moment—even the boring stuff takes on new layers. You deepen your experience of work, keep things fun, and also find more openings to success. Opportunities to be more present and available are everywhere.

For example, the divisional head of the San Francisco office and I had sons about the same age who were both interested in baseball. He approached me and asked if I would be his assistant coach on a Little League team in the neighborhood where we lived. For him there was the practical side. We both traveled a lot for work. Being with the same firm and servicing largely the same clientele, our team would never be without a coach since he and I rarely traveled together. I accepted the offer and became a Little League coach. Now you might be cynical and suspect that of course I would do whatever the boss suggested as a way of ingratiating myself. That would be the cynic's response. But my reason was quite different: I wanted the experience of it.

The success of the team and working with these young boys became the primary focus and benefit of our coaching experience. My boss and I learned a lot about each other and how we dealt with challenging situations. We also shared in the joy of our little team winning games they were not expected to. The experience was just plain fun and was a great relief from the pressures of our office jobs. I learned a lot about working with competitive boys and making sure everyone was given a chance. I learned about teaching the boys to support each other and to value the importance of the whole and not just the individual. The other benefit was associating fun with my work experience and deepening my relationship with my boss. With this simple act of cooperation, I was able to add a new level of enjoyment in my work life and to add time with my family.

I like to think of creating a positive experience as adding variety and nuance to the day-to-day activities that can often dominate the normal work experience. The more you can add variation, the more interested and interesting you become. I do my best to approach the moment

Present and Available

with the question, how can I make this mean something? And sometimes, that attention sets waterfalls in motion that create real value in the world.

When I meet people, I often think, *Who else might want to know them?* I had the opportunity to meet the then president of the World Wildlife Fund. Knowing that a partner of mine at Goldman had a passionate interest in preserving the Amazon rainforest, I introduced the two of them. This partner became instrumental in developing a critical plan and worldwide document for an organization pivotal in preserving large parts of the Amazon. Being present and open to connecting people from differing silos of your universe makes you an important component in the process of solution thinking. My openness to the possibilities made something important happen.

It's not all about big stuff, though. There's a lot of possibility and enjoyment in the little things—that's what makes up most of our days. Remembering a client's birthday or sending them a new article of interest are actions that brought more positivity to my working days. One thing I like about my phone is it reminds me of someone's birthday, and when I get the reminder, I send a text. The incredible result is the recipient is usually surprised and always responds—almost as if no one else had remembered their birthday. For me this has become a thoughtful expression that creates another avenue of conversation with my client. First, this simple act demonstrates my interest in them. Second, it brings more nuance to my business relationships as we venture into more personal territory. Finally, it creates an

CONNECTABILITY

opportunity for conversation, which generally leads to a positive business result.

It seems clear to me that if I cannot bring balance into my life, I won't be very interesting or interested. If you care about something and share your enthusiasm and joy, your relationships and clients will experience positivity as well. Treat the moments in your day as opportunities for discovery, and see what you can find in them. Doing so will set you apart from others.

One story that illustrates the importance of being present and available has nothing to do with my work in sales. However, it does demonstrate its importance, underscoring the value of extending appreciation to others even when there appears to be no benefit. Life has a way of providing an opportunity to receive when you have been able to give.

It was the morning of 9/11, and I was set to travel across the country from New York City to San Francisco like I did every week in that period of my life. I'd just dropped my kids off at school before heading to the airport, where I checked in and sat down to wait for my flight.

After a few minutes, I looked at the TV and saw footage of a plane crashing into the World Trade Center. As I tried to process what I was seeing, one of the attendants working there—a woman I often saw and took time to speak with—approached me.

"Fred," she said, "all flights are canceled and the airport is closing. You have to leave. I've rented you the very last car."

She handed me the keys and I made it to the rental car

Present and Available

lot, where I saw one solitary vehicle. I drove it to Long Island. As the crisis of the day unfolded, I was able to get out of the airport, make it to a phone, and call my family, letting them know the hijacked flight to San Francisco wasn't mine and that I was okay. I was able to do this as soon as I did because a woman I didn't know very well, but who always took time to warmly connect with me for the simple reason that we were both humans sharing an interaction, chose me to rent the last car. I remain thankful. It remains true for me that small outward extensions are rewarded in ways we may not immediately see. The habit of being present and available at all times when interacting with other humans can end up reaping unexpected benefits.

After I sold my ranch, I spent some time living in a small apartment on a dock facing the San Francisco Bay as I took some time finding my next home. My simple ritual while living there was to get up early and walk a few steps to an Italian coffee shop for a cappuccino at the beginning of the day. Becoming a regular was a truly pleasant way to begin the day, and by paying attention—being present and available—I began to learn a little more about the owners' and other customers' lives. I also came to notice that Friday mornings, the refuse was picked up from the restaurants and small businesses in my neighborhood.

Garbage pickup is one of those necessary jobs that we're aware of but often don't engage with very much. But I found myself witnessing it every Friday as I ventured out in my morning ritual. I had a choice. Walk by, maneuver around, or be present and engage. I chose to engage.

CONNECTABILITY

It turned out the man operating the truck and collecting the refuse had a big personality. As the weeks progressed, we engaged more and more with each other. Sometimes his son would work with him, and I got to know him too. I learned where they lived, that this was his last stop of his day, where he was born, and on and on. I think we both looked forward to our once-a-week interaction as we developed a friendship outside of our "tribes."

In a way that's hard to describe, there is real richness in coming to know people outside the usual silos we so often keep ourselves locked in. On top of this, making this new friend enlivened my walk to the coffee shop. A final benefit came in a conversation one normal Friday. My friend, who learned a lot while picking up the trash every week, told me of a home that was coming on the market but had not yet been listed. This was during the pandemic, a period of time in the Bay Area when homes, especially outside the city, were hard to come by. This simple heads-up gave me an early look at a home I eventually bought.

So often, we stay on the path we expect or want—which is often the quickest way to our destination. Yet when we stay present and available to the path that is opening in front of us—taking off the blinders that keep us focused on only what *we* want from the world—we receive in new ways.

Our preconceived assumptions may be well-thought-out and even defensible, but they can prevent us from seeing opportunities. I find a greater return, both in sales and my personal life, when I remember to be present and available to what is at hand—at a red light, in conversation with my server over the wine list, talking to a loved one, chatting with the man operating the garbage truck on my street, or checking out at the grocery store. These moments all have gifts to give, when I extend myself to give and receive them. Bringing this attitude, discipline, and practice is a great way to deepen your relationship building.

Being present and available allows you to take relationships beyond the merely transactional and instead fill them with human nuance—which will differentiate you from most of your competition and bring those relationships to another level of success.

Good leaders are by definition present for others to emulate and available to help those around them. The example that you set through your availability will distinguish you from others and will set you on a pathway of leadership. Let's explore how becoming a leader is all about the example you set and your availability to guide others through that example.

CHAPTER 7

Leadership

I arrived at 85 Broad Street on a warm June morning. It was my first day at Goldman Sachs.

My journey did not happen in a traditional fashion. There was no MBA recruiting and no internship. Instead, a not-so-well-thought-out business plan had resulted in my decision to leave an asset management venture at the same time a good friend of mine was looking for an experienced salesperson to fill the fixed-income sales desk in the Goldman San Francisco office. After a series of interviews, I was offered a job at the prestigious investment bank, in the same building I had started my career several years earlier.

The opportunity was a good example of the importance of maintaining relationships even if there seems to be no

CONNECTABILITY

immediate benefit. It was also another example of the axiom that when one door closes, another opens. It proved the start of an amazing adventure and opportunity for me.

After accepting the job offer in the San Francisco office, I landed in New York City for training, where I began the process of new-hire orientation, introductions, and assimilation into the Goldman methodology and structure. At the time, Wall Street firms were concentrated in a small area of lower Manhattan where you could feel the dynamic nature of the business on every street. The Goldman offices were impressive in that traditional old-school way, which to me felt important.

My orientation was on an executive floor with dark wood paneling and furniture, and an ambiance that I can only describe as very East Coast. I was ushered into the room with other fresh-faced young professionals—although to be honest, I was not exactly a fresh face. As mentioned, I was not a traditional hire and would always be the oldest one in my class. As we waited for the senior partners to arrive and address this new class of employees, I still felt fresh, though, and a little nervous. As a new hire I couldn't help but wonder if they had made a mistake. While I was nervous, I also felt I deserved to be there. There is no doubt I was excited about this opportunity. I would make sure they never felt they had made a mistake.

At the time there was no casual Friday—that wouldn't come until a decade later, when Wall Street was competing with Silicon Valley to hire newly minted MBAs. On this June morning, a dark suit and tie were the order of the day,

Leadership

and so I sat with the others around a large table, dressed for the part, and waited for one or both of the senior partners to appear.

John L. Weinberg and John C. Whitehead had become co-senior partners of the firm a few years before my arrival. The firm had a culture of shared leadership, with the partners often selecting two individuals to jointly head the firm. For Goldman, this was another way to demonstrate the importance of the firm's cultural values of teamwork and collaboration.

When John Weinberg entered the room to speak to this group of new employees, the first thing I noticed was how he carried himself. There was a different aura around this man people regarded as a titan of Wall Street—one of ease and familiarity. He was relaxed, humble, and welcoming, not at all like the typical high-strung Wall Street type so often characterized in the media. He sat down in a chair to speak with us rather than standing over us. It was like a favorite uncle had come to talk to you about how your dating life was going. When his partner John Whitehead joined us, he entered the room in an equally unassuming manner, although in a slightly more sophisticated, erudite style.

Together, these two men displayed a kindness and understanding unlike any other leaders I had been exposed to. Sitting around that table with us, they didn't talk about making money, and they didn't talk about the greatness of the firm or themselves. Instead, they spoke about being a good team member, about helping and assisting our colleagues in conducting business, and most importantly, about the firm's clients. They acknowledged that these clients made the firm money but emphasized that Goldman was interested in client relationships for the long term. They spoke about understanding client needs and meeting those with the best the firm had to offer.

Weinberg and Whitehead also acknowledged the importance of family and balance. Finally, they spoke of reputation and its importance to both the firm and to us as individuals as we went about building our own reputations.

As they talked about serving and listening to their clients, they were instilling a sense of leadership through their belief system. Through this system of client first and firm second, they asked all of us to be leaders by adhering to a code of ethics and principles. We would individually lead the colleagues who were working around us.

As different in style as these two men were, their message was perfectly blended—and powerful. Even this first introduction to the firm was a lesson in leadership by example as they also built a leadership credo: one centered in client service, listening, knowledge, reputation, and service to community. They were, in truth, building a core of employees who all could be leaders and lead people around them. At the time, we didn't know we were leaders. After all, we were new hires and didn't have the title to claim it. But as these two men spoke, we realized that it wasn't about the title. If we maintained the principles being laid out, we would be the leaders they needed to build the organization they envisioned.

Leadership

As my time at Goldman continued, I only grew in respect for the partnership of the "two Johns," as they were affectionately known. These two gentlemen exemplified the best qualities of the firm and led by example in all aspects, both personal and professional. They were incredible leaders but not in the style that we see on the big screen or in media today. They taught me much of what I know of leadership.

We can all be leaders. The two Johns knew this. Sure, they did more typical top-down leadership things (and did them well). I still remember the list of fourteen business principles Whitehead crafted that would define Goldman as it grew into the world's dominant investment bank. But in addition, they created multiple leaders throughout the firm. They exemplified the truth that great leaders are inclusive, thoughtful, and empathetic and work together with their colleagues to achieve great results. Good leaders are visible to their employees, especially in crisis. The good leaders of the firm "walked the floor" in good times as well as challenging times so employees could interact with them and see they were present and available. They made every effort to understand and work with people of different backgrounds and modes of thought. The mere fact that they shared the leadership position demonstrated the value of teamwork and shared goals.

Certainly, there were people who contributed more to the revenue of the firm, but what was rewarded was the ability to work together to achieve that revenue. Goldman was not an organization built around stars; it was an organization

CONNECTABILITY

built around an idea: serving clients and defending the firm's reputation. We knew we had nothing if we didn't have our reputation. The two Johns knew that if they could create a culture of teamwork, they could create the foundation for everything else.

As an extension of this teamwork culture, I rarely went on a call with a client alone. I always took someone else from the firm, and through this my clients felt they had access to all the brilliant minds available at the firm. I wanted my clients to know that I could get them in front of any colleague we thought would be of value. It wasn't about paying lip service to teamwork. It was deeply embedded in our culture of leadership, and people were compensated for their efforts to work together to achieve desired outcomes for the firm and its clients. The leadership of the firm leveraged that culture in a way rarely replicated.

Somehow as a society we have come to see leadership in a narrow manner—as a singular person leading a team of people. This style of leadership would not have served the Goldman firm as well. Under the leadership of the two Johns, we at Goldman did not see a singular individual leading the charge. We saw multiple leaders with shared values working together, and it encouraged all of us to become a leader in our own right.

You do not have to be anointed to be a leader. You can lead by setting an example. You can lead by applying what you have learned in the chapters of this book. Leadership is doing, not following, and it doesn't have a whole lot to do with what your title is. Leadership is acquired by setting an

Leadership

example and following through with that example. And it is demonstrated every day through your applied activities.

Certainly, there are many aspects to being a good leader, and plenty of books written about them. While many of these have value, I want to focus now on leadership by example, a type of leadership that can start well before ever being anointed as a leader. Part of leading by example is being consistent, first in your ability to set a positive example in your principles and second in the message you give through your performance.

My experience with philanthropic institutions and universities underscores the benefits of leading by example. For a number of years, I was the chairman of the University of California at Santa Barbara Foundation Board. We would meet twice a year at one of the ten campuses of the UC system. The year I was first appointed chairman, I attended a meeting of the other nine chairmen at UC Irvine. The college had just hired a new dean to head up their growing business school, and because of the growing medical research on the Irvine campus, the business school was focused on the business of medicine. The new head of the business school had just arrived from the University of Wisconsin, and that day he was the keynote speaker at our group's luncheon. His speech was focused on how he would be working with his board of directors.

Different chief executives have various styles when it comes to working with a board. Some seem to keep their boards at arm's length. They know they need to have a board but either don't want to use them or don't know how to use them. Some, like the new head of the business school, feel otherwise and see their boards as assets. Like the two Johns, this leader saw the benefit of teamwork and wanted his board to be a working board. Most importantly, he wanted the board to understand his message and be able to articulate that message to others. He expected his board members to have prepared reports when they had meetings. The expectation was for his board members to know what the school's priorities were and what his message as dean was to his constituency, so they could share it in times when he wasn't present. In other words, he wanted his board members to be leaders in their own right and to lead not only by example but also by action.

I found this an inspiring message, especially as I'd been on several boards that seemed to serve in name only. I knew that organizations are far more powerful and effective if those in leadership roles are acting in concert with each other. Our efforts are much more powerful when they are amplified by the people around us. Protecting turf or insulating your clients from your teammates not only shortchanges your clients but also limits your effectiveness. You are not in control of what your boss thinks or what the company decides as a strategy. But you are in control of what you do and how you connect. How you work with your clients and colleagues is entirely under your own leadership. Your growing success in building relationships will make you a leader people look up to for help and advice.

I would say the best way to get to this place of recognition is through recognizing you aren't meant to be the star

Leadership

on your own. Effective leaders are team leaders. They lead by bringing everyone on the team up with them, in a way that elevates the team beyond simply an easy buzzword. You can do this on your own whether or not your organization promotes it, when you lead by example, collaborate, and help lift the people around you to their highest potential.

The success of the team is always greater than the success of one, and it is the success of the whole, not of the individual parts, that makes a client relationship experience superior results.

Along with teamwork and consistency, positivity is another foundational block for good leadership. I want to follow a leader who is seeking positive solutions to problems. The negative is always the easiest to develop. The problem with that is the solution is never found. I want my clients to know I will always endeavor to find a solution. If my answer is to belittle my competition or find someone else to blame, I'm not focusing on the solution; rather, I am searching for an excuse. That process leaves the problem unsolved and the client unhappy. Demonstrating the ability to find a positive solution rather than digging into the negative will signal to others that you are a leader to follow, as well as bring everyone more collective success.

Leaders also share deep presence with the people around them, regardless of how important they may be. I remember when I introduced the senior partners of the firm to my clients at the Kamehameha Schools. In spite of all the things they had to attend to at any given time, they were each always completely focused on the conversation in front of them. The message to the client was: You are important. I remember feeling that level of importance from my meetings. It gave us all confidence and the encouragement we needed to live up to those high expectations. This is exactly what you want to do as a leader.

In every way, the leadership and legacy of the two Johns was generosity. I strove to become equally generous, both in my own individual leadership throughout my career and also in my approach to life. That's why I believe one more essential component to being a strong leader is to also be a good steward.

When I owned the ranch, my principal goal was to be a good steward of the land. When I purchased the property, I knew that in reality, I was just a guardian for the moment rather than an owner, as the property surely would outlast me. I was determined to leave it in better shape than when I found it. I believe I did exactly that. When I sold it, the creek beds were vibrant with willows, sycamores, and oak trees; the grass was full enough to choke out the weeds. Buildings occupied less than 1 percent of the property. The native animals of California sought refuge there, as there was plenty of water and forage.

When building a relationship, viewing yourself as a steward of that relationship will create a sense of ownership that transcends the mere transactional. By thinking of yourself as a responsible steward, you can move away from self and instead be a leader for others. Envisioning myself as a caretaker for my business relationships allows me to prioritize the client. When we complete successful transactions, they

Leadership

will be more client-oriented. I'll be thinking of preserving and building my team as well.

Through the lens of stewardship, I remain focused on leaving the relationship in a better place. I remain focused on generosity.

Which brings us to our next chapter.

CHAPTER 8

Generosity

Transactions can often be the focus as you are initially building a business. However, a transaction is a fleeting success. The real success is the relationship enduring over time. An important building block of a lasting relationship is the level of generosity you exhibit as you build.

Success is about bringing your humanity and generosity into your relationships. Companies and the relationships that build them are founded on the generosity shown to each other. Those who are willing to extend themselves are demonstrating their interest in fostering a great client experience. The depth of the relationship often rises from the depth of your generosity to another person, regardless of the amount of business you are transacting.

CONNECTABILITY

As I've shared, one of my favorite restaurants is Bell's. I've also shared that Bell's was able to survive the Covid pandemic through changing their business model. What I haven't mentioned yet is that Daisy and Greg Ryan not only survived, but through it all, they also made giving to others a priority. Their focus was not only on providing an amazing customer experience but also on bringing their authenticity and generosity to all.

The margins in the restaurant business are not huge. As a matter of fact, compared to most businesses they are small. When you are starting out, there's not much room for error—being generous can be challenging even when you want to be. Add to that the challenges of staying afloat through a pandemic and countrywide shutdown. Daisy and Greg were not ones to shrink from a challenge. They were determined to survive, while also supporting the community they lived and worked in.

Although Santa Barbara County—the home of Bell's—is considered a wealthy county, revenue comes primarily through agriculture, which means the Central Coast is also home to many agricultural workers. In spite of the area's wealth, this is a community of some food insecurity. With the arrival of the pandemic, the needs of this community became greater.

With a new baby and a recently opened restaurant, the Ryans had their hands full, but regardless of these challenges, they demonstrated that generosity does not have to come only from the well-heeled or firmly established. Thankful that their employees were loyal and the

Generosity

community had come to support them when they needed it, the Ryans started the Feed the Valley organization. The idea was to provide meals on a weekly basis to those most in need in the local community. They knew they couldn't provide enough meals on their own, so they took on the additional task of convincing other restaurants to participate. They managed to convince thirty restaurants to join their philanthropic model, which became a highly successful collaboration.

This was an exceptional demonstration of generosity, as the Ryans gave of their time, intellectual capital, and inspiration while taking a business risk. Beyond the material resources needed to develop and sustain the program, a lot of energy was required to make this happen.

Generosity comes in different packages. As I see it, there are seven forms of generosity I find deeply meaningful: sharing our thoughts, words, time, influence, attention, money, and possessions. Many people think of money first, and there are plenty of good examples of people being incredibly generous with their wealth. But it's just one way to give. It's also a form of giving that can sometimes be what I would call false generosity—generosity with conditions attached, giving to exert control over someone. Furthermore, it's not the most enduring form of generosity when building sustainable sales relationships with integrity and honesty.

In our work in sales, we want to be present and available through sincere generosity. Demonstrating one's ability to be generous in an all-encompassing way establishes a personal reputation of giving. This is generosity without expectation.

CONNECTABILITY

Yet the truth is, generosity like this often returns to us. What is interesting about generosity is how many of the qualities we have been discussing play a role in its development. The Ryans had to be empathetic to learn and understand what was needed, who needed it, and how to provide it. All of this had to be done in a way that allowed all parties to maintain their dignity. Daisy and Greg listened to community organizers and stakeholders and to their collaborators to hear what would work for both the restaurants and those in need. They took risks, both reputational risk and the opportunity for financial loss (in a situation where there were no overt rewards).

Many philanthropic organizations don't take the time to truly understand how all these elements play into generosity or to understand what their constituency needs or desires. I saw this lack of understanding when I was involved with university fundraising. Often a university is entirely focused on a project, like a new building or lab, rather than the interest of the potential benefactor. The project becomes the overwhelming focus. Reorienting the approach would be to establish the interest of the potential benefactor through questions and listening. Once you have established their level of interest, then you can craft "an ask" that resonates in a meaningful way.

In many ways, giving back is similar to the first sales meeting. I cannot expect to sell my product in the first meeting. My real goal is the second meeting. And in that same way, philanthropic fundraising is best when you are more focused on trying to establish a long-term relationship

Generosity

than simply getting what you want for a given project. I watched many times when a philanthropic organization did not take the time to listen to what a benefactor—and their spouse—was interested in. I watched one such mistake where a husband and wife wished to give a gift to a university. The university was raising money for a new building. The development officer focused his attention on the husband, instead of also inquiring about the wife's interests. Ultimately the couple donated $2 million for the building but gave a whopping $50 million to a small liberal arts school that focused on religious studies. The irony was that the university raising money for the building was considered the number one school for religious studies. Situations like this underscore the importance of empathetic inquiry and attentive listening.

The development officer would have been well served to also remember that generosity is not a transaction. Generosity to your stakeholders is a deep understanding of not only your needs but theirs as well.

There's an African philosophy that expresses this well: *ubuntu*. I had never heard of this word until I had coffee with a woman who was a coach and lecturer on the value of human communication. She'd reached out to me, as we share a similar philosophy: We both value communication through direct personal interaction so that all nuance is present—voice intonation, inflection, feeling, body language, and facial expression.

When she first reached out, I had a choice of ignoring the message or stepping out of my comfort zone or friendship zone to make myself available. I made the right choice. And I learned something wonderful and new.

Ubuntu is an African philosophy that places the emphasis on "being self through others." It is a form of humanism that can be expressed in the phrase "I am because of who we all are."

This philosophy helps us understand we are part of a whole. I am because of the contributions of others. The more others I allow to enter my consciousness, the broader and more empathetic I myself can become. This philosophy helps us approach the truest form of generosity, the giving of ourselves, because we are all part of a greater whole, together.

Approaching relationships with this thought in mind will help you build the kind of long-term, sustainable relationship you are searching for. I cannot stress enough how the quick sale is a sure way to an ephemeral relationship. Instead, take the time to learn and listen to your new relationship. Be generous with who you are. With this kind of generosity and understanding, you also become more open to hearing another opinion, which will almost always serve you and the world.

I was reminded of this principle one afternoon when I went for a walk with an extraordinary friend of mine. It was my first hike following my knee surgery, and we'd just experienced torrential rains in Marin County. The streams and waterfalls were spectacular, as the mountains had become temporary rainforests. We tend to cover many important subjects on these walks, and on this one we talked of the silos we have managed to put ourselves in. Either socially

Generosity

or politically, we are all now identified with one group or another. It then becomes hard to get out of any of these boxes, and we are generally identified as being a member of a certain tribe or belief system. For instance, if you are socially conscious, you are a liberal and assigned the moniker of "woke." If you are conservative, you are labeled MAGA, with all its attributes. One comment my friend made has stuck with me: "If I cannot understand your belief system, how can I possibly expect to teach you about mine, much less convince you of my relevance?"

This openness to understanding and tolerating is an important aspect of generosity. "I want to listen to you." That simple expression of empathy is the greatest door opener of all that we have been discussing. When you are building a relationship, think about how generous you can be in ways beyond material transactions. You will separate yourself from your competition if you can generously extend yourself beyond the product you are selling. Since we are building relationships, we are always looking for ways to distinguish ourselves from others. Offering yourself without the expectation of reciprocation is hard to do. Think of the powerful relationship you can build if your counterpart understands that you have more to offer than merely contractual success. In the broadest terms, you achieve this by asking, how can *I* help *you*?

One evening, I was with a small group of friends and we'd stopped on our way to dinner at a Western apparel hat store in Vail. The store was unusually busy, and since we knew the two women who were trying to deal with this

CONNECTABILITY

crush of customers, one of my pals and I started to help people explore the store. It turned into a hilariously fun experience and act of generosity, as my friend and I can be quite entertaining, and our store friends really needed help. For us, it was simple: We gave time and were willing to take some social risk. But when it comes to building relationships, it is not the size of the help that usually matters—but the sincerity, selflessness, and intention behind it. I want to take myself out of what I am comfortable with and make myself available to others in an act of generosity without transactional expectation.

Another form of generosity I've witnessed is the simple act of celebrating each other and affirming the relationship. This idea first came to my attention while watching my ten-year-old granddaughter play volleyball with her teammates. She is a member of a group of uniquely gifted young women playing the sport, and aside from their prowess on the court, what I noticed was the camaderie of the team. After every single point, they met in the middle of the court to touch hands and prepare for the next point. It was a quick but powerful act of affirmation—of their support for each other, their skills, and their friendships. With this renewed strength, they were better prepared for the next point.

I saw this once more when I had lunch the other day with a dear friend, and the customers at two tables near us caught my attention. These two groups of women were each celebrating the birthday of one of their friends. I find that women are especially good at celebrating important events and supporting their friends through a crisis. Such

Generosity

affirmation of each other and the relationship is an act of generosity that deepens connection.

Generosity of spirit is truly thinking of someone else first. And it's not especially common. One day while driving, I turned right onto a two-lane road and immediately noticed that a young woman had stopped her car in her traffic lane and was running to assist an older woman who had tripped and fallen off the curbed sidewalk. She had stopped and jumped out of her car to help this older woman to her feet, without regard for the cars behind her or her own safety. As I looked for a place to park so I could get out and assist, I saw the woman two cars back from the scene of the fallen woman. She was clearly perturbed that something was holding up traffic and causing her to now be delayed for some important event... And another thought crossed my mind: What is the character trait that causes an individual to take a risk for the potential benefit of someone else? What makes a person willing to give of themselves to help others?

Caring is often acknowledged warmly but in a way that underscores how unique it is. We expect and are not surprised at the behavior of the woman two cars back—angry and self-important, upset that the world had bothered to delay her. On a corporate level, generosity can also be linked to brand experience. When building relationships, you are building your own brand, and that brand can be a richer experience when you successfully bring your passion to your clients' experience. As you grow your network of stakeholders and clients, you can strengthen that bond

CONNECTABILITY

through generosity. Continually ask yourself, how can I do better, how can I deepen this connection, and how can I make this relationship more rewarding for my client? This kind of generosity builds long-lasting and successful relationships.

Don't seek out the self-serving opportunity. Just be generous and then equally open to receive. If you can embrace the ubuntu idea that "I am because of who we all are," you will become more open to the idea of being generous in a variety of ways. You don't learn much or expand your horizons if you don't extend yourself. Generosity is sincerity and openness, the willingness to give of oneself when it is comfortable and also when it is not. Take yourself out of the box to expose yourself to learning something new and being of greater service.

Here is one final story on the power of generosity. In my small town of Sausalito, Monika and Alessandro, a young Italian couple, opened a pizzeria, Sandrino. They have a large local following, as their product is outstanding. Sausalito is also a town that experiences a small community of homeless people, and one such man often walks by Sandrino. Instead of asking this gentleman to leave, Monika and Alessandro give him a table and serve him as a guest at their restaurant. One busy Friday evening, a couple waiting to have a table open up suggested they take the table occupied by the homeless man eating his dinner. Monika kindly told the impatient couple that tables were on a first-come, first-served basis and they respected all of their patrons, not just the ones who had homes. Alessandro and Monika

Generosity

continue to offer this homeless gentleman a meal whenever he comes. Their generosity is known throughout the community, and their business continues to thrive.

Thinking in terms of how you can assist others will deepen the relationships you are trying to build. And then take it one step further, and be an advocate for generosity.

Act without regard to self and see what happens. These stories of generosity and its importance have a similar characteristic: They all require consistent follow-up. The one-time gift may be valuable; however, the consistency demonstrated by following up underscores not only the sincerity with which it is given but also the enduring benefit of follow-up. In our next chapter, we will explore the critical skill of following up in all aspects of relationship building.

CHAPTER 9

Follow-Up

"It takes months to find a customer and only seconds to lose one." "The fortune is in the follow-up." A couple of well-known quotes not attributed to anyone in particular both echo the same reality: Not following up with your prospect is the same as trying to fill up your bathtub without first putting the stopper in the drain. When building your relationships, following up is perhaps the easiest way to make them fruitful and long-lasting. Yet it is the one act that is so often ignored or forgotten.

I have learned much from my experience of training horses, including when that time on my ranch came to an end. It was a sad closing chapter for me, but one that taught me a great deal about patience and follow-up,

CONNECTABILITY

both of which are unique and critical parts of developing relationships.

After selling the ranch, and my Ford truck with it, I moved to the northern part of California. I sought to find myself a vehicle more suited to my now-urban life and one day walked into a high-end auto dealership with this purpose. A couple of salesmen—I specifically want to point out they were men—were sitting around their desks, seemingly intent on scrolling on their phones. After several minutes of perusing, no one approached me. I was surprised—they didn't seem particularly interested in finding out why I was in their showroom.

Eventually, a salesman approached me and asked what I was looking for. I told him I was interested in a particular model but wasn't familiar with the various options. What would be best for my type of driving? The salesman told me I could go on the brand's website and build my own, and once I had completed this, I could call him and he'd find out if the car was available. He handed me his card. I then volunteered my name and number, although he had not specifically asked for it.

I looked at the build-your-own website, but I did not know how the various options added to the value of the car or the performance. In other words, I could have used a little commentary, and as I had asked, I could have used an opinion. The assumption that I would be all knowledgeable already is a mistake in many sales circumstances. Assumption is a dangerous form of opinion since it is formed without proof. In sales and relationship building,

Follow-Up

assuming is also a sure way to fail in your goal. If a client knows the answer, they will tell you, but don't presume they know. Finding out what they need to know is a good way of building and forming a positive relationship.

In this case, directing me to a build-your-own website without follow-up was a sure way to not make the sale. The salesman never called and neither did I, thus ending the relationship. A year later, I had an entirely different experience when I decided to investigate purchasing a new Subaru (the make of car I eventually landed on after my move north). I had taken my older model into a dealership for service and, as part of a longer conversation, told the service manager I was interested in eventually buying a smaller hybrid model. Two days after picking up my serviced car, I received a call from a woman in the sales department, who mentioned her service rep had followed up on my interest in a smaller model with her. She asked me how she could help. To be fair, she also mentioned that there was a build-your-own option on their website—but she offered to explain the differences in model and performance options. Unlike the other salesperson a year earlier, she gave me information I could act on. She made an effort to find out what my needs were in an automobile. She listened first. And then—essentially—she followed up.

Two days after we first spoke, the rep called to see how my experience with the website had gone and if she could answer any questions. Based on the knowledge she'd obtained in our previous conversation, she now had an opinion to share with me and was prepared with the appropriate

CONNECTABILITY

knowledge. At the time, I hadn't really intended to buy a new car quite yet. But her attention to follow up was so strong that I considered buying one nonetheless.

The differences in approach between these two salespeople were striking. The first salesman displayed zero empathetic behavior. He didn't seek any information to help him determine what I was looking for or needed. He demonstrated no knowledge of the vehicle, even when, obviously, he must have known a lot. He didn't seek to demonstrate how he could add value to my search. Most importantly, he did not follow up. Not only was he not interested in being of service, but he also had no passion for his business. As little as I was impressed with his initial sales tactics (or lack thereof), following up could have cleared the air and sent a revised message. The simple act of following up would have indicated he was interested and cared.

These are two powerful messages when building a relationship where the outcome is an exchange of money for goods or service.

The second salesperson (and experience overall) was the mirror image. First, since the woman had been referred by the service group, I knew the organization worked as a team to better their business. That meant something to me. She had also done her homework. She knew what car I currently owned, and she was prepared to talk about the new model I had expressed interest in. She explained the options I'd find on the website. She displayed empathy through her listening and asking questions relating to my driving and what might work best for me.

Follow-Up

Most importantly, she followed up. She called to ask if I had managed to find the website and had been able to navigate it. She further followed up with an email outlining the car and options we had discussed. She provided all relevant information I would want, including financial information covering trade-in value and final price. Her meticulous care in following up made the entire experience seamless, pleasant, and successful. Her attention to following up underscored that initial message—we have great options for you that can meet your needs, and we truly care about you as a client.

We have all dealt with the purchase of a consumer product. The quality of the process depends not on the product but on the person selling it. And most often, it also depends on following up.

In each of our previous chapters, we've discussed essential, human-centered aspects of developing sales relationships. All of these thrive—or wither—based on following up. There is just no substitute for underscoring and extending your message by doing what you said you would do. Even if you begin a relationship grounded in all we've talked about, if you stop following up with the client, there's no longer anything there. Or if you do follow up but stop doing all you've promised, you lose trust.

If you don't follow up, all the previous chapters will be for naught. If you follow up on all that you said you would do, then the previous qualities and approaches we've discussed become amplified and more effective. The message you give to your clients (or anyone in your life)

CONNECTABILITY

is that you listen, you care, you respect their wishes, and you can be trusted. Following up doesn't just depend on the intent and desire to do so with a simple phone call; your following up will require more concentration and discipline to have impact.

One experience that has illustrated this for me, again from the client side, was when I had purchased a home and was preparing to take care of some needed repairs. I hired a contractor to oversee the project and arrange for the work to be done. One day, there was a meeting to review the progress to date and what could be expected for the next two weeks. I immediately noticed that no one was taking notes. On top of this, there was a fair amount of glancing at phones, as if to be sure no one was missing another call. As the client, I wanted to feel that an attempt was being made to remember what we were deciding upon. I did not at any point have this feeling. After an hour of reviewing various issues related to the remodel, we adjourned to go on with our day.

These meetings were held on a regular basis to keep me informed of progress and make changes as needed. Frustratingly, a recurring theme in all these meetings was that we kept having to discuss the same issues over and over. And why? It wasn't because the level of complexity required continued discussion. It was because people kept forgetting what we'd already decided and determined action around. No part of this process enabled more organized follow-up to our meetings. And so, my confidence waned. There is no easier way to derail your relationship-building efforts

Follow-Up

than repeating what has already been discussed or decided. This sort of behavior only serves to destroy confidence and demonstrate a lack of caring for the client.

Memories are understandably imperfect, as we all have many things to do. So having a method to assist and support following up is critical.

Following up requires concentration and discipline. Fortunately, many methods and tools are available that can help us remember what we said we would do for our clients and relationships. I used to carry yellow legal pads to take notes and retain important information. Today, that information can be kept digitally and is easily retrievable. Any of multiple software programs can assist you in keeping track of your follow-ups. These include tracking for number of calls, the most recent call, success rates, and so on. I would add, though, that bringing a legal pad or something you can take notes on besides a phone is still a helpful visual to show you are paying attention. I recommend taking notes and then transferring them into digital form. Utilize pen and paper and the software available to keep track of everything. All of this will build confidence during meetings and after, as it makes thorough and consistent follow-up possible. Ultimately, such tools make it possible for us to continue sending a clear, simple message: I care enough about you to do what I said I would do.

There are also many forms of digital and analog communication you can use. Of course, we're familiar with email, social media, and text—but when was the last time you received a handwritten thank-you note? These stand out for

CONNECTABILITY

three reasons. First, we don't get a lot of these anymore, so it's another way to set yourself apart. Second, a handwritten note shows you took more time. Instead of just typing out a few things on the phone and clicking "send," you have to go find a note card and a pen. Then you write the note, put on a stamp, and take it to your mailbox. It's still simple enough, but the fact that it is more of a process does register with people. Third, it's something tactile people can keep. I still have notes in my desk drawer that made an impact on me. Even if a text is powerful (and they're often not), they get buried as time passes and it's rare to remember them. A handwritten note is a powerful way to follow up. I suggest you add it to your suite of tools.

Whatever digital or analog methods you're using to follow up, another important aspect to consider and bring into your system is prioritizing. Prioritizing is a judgment call on your part. You will need to develop a list of issues that rank in priority, priorities that shift and evolve as your business and life circumstances change and evolve. For example, you might have a phone call scheduled with Client B for next month that sits at tenth on your list. However, Client B calls and leaves a message that they are interested in a recent proposal. They should now move up to your first priority by virtue of a change in circumstance. Create lists for follow-up needs by project, goals, and timing. Keep in mind that following up and prioritizing is a fluid process dictated by changing circumstances. Make sure you prioritize what you commit to, and use the tools available to help you execute.

Follow-Up

If we want to send the message that we care, forgetting is not an option. No one wants to do business or develop an ongoing relationship with someone who doesn't care and demonstrates that through their actions. The actionable item in every human interaction is following up on what you said you would do. It demonstrates commitment and affirms your abilities. In contrast, the lack of follow-up sends waves of doubt regarding both your competency and your interest in maintaining a fruitful and dynamic relationship.

Well-messaged, persistent follow-up is part of a great sales experience. And sometimes you'll need to follow up more than once. Statistics are hard to collect on this issue, but in general they tend to center on these: 80 percent of sales require an average of five follow-ups in order to close the deal. However, 44 percent of sales reps follow up with a prospect only once before giving up.[1] This is good news: It means your ability to follow up consistently will put you way ahead of the competition.

When committing to following up, there are four basic steps you'll want to incorporate:

1. Make the promise to answer the question or commit to the task.
2. Seek the information or develop the knowledge necessary to correctly perform the task.
3. Deliver a response that solves the problem or delivers knowledge to your client.

4. Reach the reward. Don't forget that you are following up on something your client or other relationship desires. There are two parties involved, so it is important to understand that you have a part in this promise to deliver. Your reward can be anything from a simple order to the more nuanced reward of a deeper and more trusted relationship.

The importance of the simple act of following up on what you committed to do regarding your relationship-building efforts cannot be overstated. Yet it can also be difficult to do. Following up requires discipline, focus, and true concern on your part to make it a habit you do not forget.

Consistency in following up relies to a large extent on habit. Much has been written on the psychology of habit formation. *Atomic Habits* by James Clear is one book I recommend; however, a number of others could inspire as well. If you need more support in creating the habit of follow-up, I suggest you explore this subject and see what resonates with you. Developing excellent follow-up as a habitual way of doing business will help increase transactions with your relationships and will also deepen trust.

Follow-up execution seems so simple on the surface. You promise to research a project. You promise to deliver on your promise. And yet, how often do we forget to execute? The sheer number of tasks that we must follow up on is one reason we often fail to complete some. However, if we focus on listening in an empathetic manner, we will be guided to better execute.

Follow-Up

I recently experienced a personal moment that brought the need and difficulty of following up into sharp focus. A good friend's father passed away, and I became aware my friend was struggling with this sad event. Having experienced a parent's death myself, I was sympathetic and wanted to reach out to him so we could meet for a chat. He was out of town for the funeral and would be returning in a week. On the surface you would think this would be the easiest thing to follow up on, yet weeks later I still had not made the call to invite him to lunch.

As I was writing this chapter on follow-up, this story came to mind. I had all the reasons in the world to make sure I extended myself to my friend to offer comfort and condolences. And still I had difficulty in execution. I'd wanted to reach out but didn't know exactly what to say. And when I didn't right away, his plight then escaped my mind. When the intention came back into focus, enough time had passed that I felt guilty, which made me more reluctant to follow up. Now too much time had passed, and I knew following up has the most impact when done in a timely manner. Nonetheless, I knew I should still do it, even if it was late.

I picked up the phone and finally invited my friend to breakfast at a familiar place that put us both at ease. I shared one of the reasons behind my slowness in reaching out: I wasn't sure if he, like me, preferred to deal with the experience of losing someone on his own. I shared with him my own unique experience with the death of my father and apologized for my insensitivity. Once I had exposed my

CONNECTABILITY

own vulnerability and let him know I was empathetic to his experience, we were able to have a lengthy conversation. The result was a deepening of our relationship.

In a business context, forgetting to follow up can be devastating to your building efforts. There is a rhythm to relationship building, starting with the first call and continuing. As previously discussed, you will not make the sale on the first call—a successful first call is meant to lead to a second and so forth. The rhythm of building will center on the development of knowledge through active listening and asking questions. Interruptions to the consistency of these recurring efforts, through forgetting to call or forgetting to follow up, will slow the process and at worst completely set you back. Someone or something will step into the void you have created by not maintaining consistency in the ritual that is becoming your relationship.

The rhythm of your relationship demands that you follow up promptly, to show your concern for your client and build trust based on your dependability. If you forget, there will almost certainly be a consequence to the relationship.

The gap created by a lack of follow-up—or perhaps as with my friend, the embarrassment of not following up—cannot be solved through continued inaction. Correct the problem immediately. The vulnerability you show in admitting you failed in whatever task was at hand will go a long way in correcting the situation, because you then expose yourself as honest and show the client you care enough to correct the problem.

I wish I had an easier answer for how to overcome the

Follow-Up

challenge of delay—it can be a difficult position. But if you find yourself in the position of needing to follow up later than you meant to, you just have to do what I did and accept you need to make the call. Accept that courage is sometimes part of building relationships. Again, being vulnerable and honest is a sure way to further build that trust and reliability that will deepen the relationship you are building.

Of all our list of relationship building blocks, following up appears to be the easiest to achieve. But it is actually the most difficult. Part of the reason is the list of tasks to follow up on grows every day. It all seems so simple when we think about it. But like with so many things, the challenge is in the doing. To help you, build out the tools that will assist you in remembering all the things you have committed to. Digital tools are a good support mechanism to keep you current.

Following up is truly the building block that makes all the others stronger. It delivers a powerful message to your client or your friend—anyone with whom you're developing a relationship. There is just no other way that says loud and clear that you were listening and are acting on the information you have learned.

And remember, when you fail in this way, be vulnerable enough to admit it and acknowledge your mistake. Is this easy? No. But being vulnerable is never easy. And in ways that go far beyond follow-up, it's valuable to our relationships—something I'm realizing more and more.

Let's dig into this countercultural idea of vulnerability next.

CHAPTER 10

Vulnerability

I've been thinking about what characteristic is deeply essential but not as obvious in the building of deep, long-lasting business relationships. I've come to the idea of vulnerability, which in all honesty is for me still a work in progress. Yet I know it's work worth doing.

When I was writing about risk, I came to understand that a real skill to building long-lasting relationships is that of making oneself vulnerable. When I think of this in the context of business relationships, I don't mean becoming vulnerable as in weak, or completely exposed to potential attack, but rather as a level of openness that makes one available for a truly deep and rewarding relationship. The vulnerability of taking the risk to expose yourself to being

CONNECTABILITY

known and reach a true understanding. You can do this while also doing your best to protect yourself.

When we consider vulnerability, we need to explore nuances. Whether people think of vulnerability as a negative or a positive, it's generally regarded as a place of powerlessness. I say the concept is more complex. I don't confuse vulnerability with weakness. I think we can be both vulnerable and retain strength.

My work with horses exemplifies this concept. Horses are large animals, somewhat unpredictable and certainly powerful, thus leaving us at a physical disadvantage and therefore vulnerable to harm, as vulnerability is often defined and understood. I could be vulnerable training a twelve-hundred-pound animal, but that does not mean that I am weak. If I am weak or allow the horse to sense weakness, then we could never learn from each other and our relationship would break down.

What does it mean to be vulnerable but not weak with a horse? It means that you retain control. You've trained. You have saddles, you have spurs, you have a bit, you have reins. You've prepared and are utilizing tools that give you strength. You want the horse to know you are the boss. Horses need to know that the rider is confident in the outcome. You cannot demonstrate fear, as that exhibits a lack of confidence. Yet you are vulnerable—you can still be bucked off. But while you still take on risk, you enter the space in a position of strength, with the tools you need.

Dealing with horses by definition puts you in a vulnerable position, and this acceptance of vulnerability is what allows

Vulnerability

for growth and success. You're allowing yourself to be open to new learning and achieving—you cannot do what the horse can do, therefore you must be open to how they receive your instructions. You must learn to "speak" to them in a manner of their choosing. Through the acceptance of this positioning, you can achieve a level of deep understanding and successful communication. This deep understanding that can grow allows for deeper success.

Vulnerability is an opportunity to grow as a person and find satisfaction in our relationships. Often when building a new relationship, we come with our protective shields in place. We demonstrate our knowledge by talking and not listening. We allow our egos to dominate the conversation. We fear rejection, and so we keep more of ourselves closed off. But by opening into vulnerability and a willingness to trust and stand in our authentic selves, we foster empathy and a stronger bond. When you embrace vulnerability, you show trust in the other person, and you encourage them to trust you in turn. In the end, good relationship building requires trust. I would rather have trust than high performance in the building of long-term, successful relationships.

As I wrote in our chapter on leadership, on my very first day at Goldman, John Weinberg talked about trust and the firm's reputation. He felt it was the firm's most valuable asset, and without it, the firm had no business. It was also a vulnerable asset and one that needed constant attention. The firm's most important asset—its reputation—lived within its vulnerability. Your reputation is your most valuable and critical asset, and being vulnerable builds the trust that builds your reputation.

As I often do, I consulted a thesaurus to look for synonyms for vulnerable. As expected, most of them we would consider as having a more negative connotation. However, three of them—accessible, exposed, out on a limb[1]—grabbed my attention, as they pertain to the positive aspects of building relationships.

I want to be accessible to my clients. Accessibility will lead them to come to me when they need my assistance. Being exposed means I am bringing my true self to a relationship, which allows honest communication and leads to the foundational element of trust. Finally, going out on a limb for my clients is also a good way to build trust and show my clients I have their best interest at the forefront of my efforts.

A number of antonyms to vulnerable—immune, impervious, well protected—are also revealing, in the sense that they are not necessarily things that generally lead to a valued and enduring association. I do not want to be immune in building relationships, as progress and development will only come by being receptive. If I am impervious, what can I receive? And if I'm impervious to your feelings or needs, I cannot be open to hearing what would help me to be more effective. Certainly, being well protected might feel safe and secure, but it certainly does not leave any openings for the conversation that leads to a value-added transaction.

Being vulnerable may seem difficult, even out of place, in building business relationships. However, it tends to

Vulnerability

reduce anxiety, build self-awareness, and create stronger connections. Remember, your ability to be vulnerable gives your partner or business associate permission to do the same. You show strength by showing you are aware of your vulnerabilities. You can always bring in people who are more skilled at concepts that don't come to you naturally. Knowing where you are vulnerable makes you better able to serve your clients.

Even the challenges of problem-solving are helped by your willingness to be vulnerable. There is a lack of credibility when you insist on always being correct. At some point, this lack of honest acknowledgment of where you can improve will come back to weaken your efforts to build and be connected.

Of course, the value of vulnerability also extends to our personal relationships. While these personal relationships differ from business relationships in terms of how vulnerable we might want to allow ourselves to become, they still illuminate the power of vulnerability.

I wrote a blog post[2] recently talking about friendships and the surprisingly fleeting nature of many of them. When I was in college, I thought my friends would be my friends forever. But a few years after graduation, my remaining college friendships had dwindled to just a few. Likewise, when I was in my multiple-decade career in the securities industry, I thought the people I worked with every day, both colleagues and clients, would remain in my life forever.

Now as the years have flown by, the number of colleagues I am still close to has been reduced. While I

CONNECTABILITY

cultivated deep and powerful business relationships that extended in valuable ways through my financial services career, now that I've moved from the industry, I have very few previous client relationships that have stood the test of time. At the same time, I have observed some of my colleagues who have been able to maintain client relationships years after their business concluded. I've also watched some others—notably, some of the closest women in my life—maintain friendships from their elementary school days, across decades and wide physical distance. My daughter has a friend she has known since the two were born three doors apart in a small community north of San Francisco. To this day they are lifelong best friends. She has many close relationships she's carried forward with her, through life transitions and time.

I recently asked myself why I hadn't carried as many old connections forward into the future, across evolving life paths. I now believe the difference lies in the ability to be vulnerable. While I conducted business with them regularly, those relationships retained a certain guardedness that left them more fragile and ephemeral.

My years in the Goldman office in San Francisco were characterized by closer, more vulnerable relationships. I became far more guarded when I transferred to the New York office as national sales manager. Working in the San Francisco office was the high point of my career at Goldman. It was with an amazing collection of thoughtful, kind professionals who had a genuine interest in and friendship with their colleagues. Many colleagues from that close-knit

Vulnerability

office remain close friends. We were competitive, but with other firms rather than with each other, and therefore the office ran super smoothly—a legacy I inherited from my boss and one I like to think I continued when I became the office manager.

We shared a significant level of friendship and vulnerability in our office, and I had expected the same when I moved to be the national sales manager in New York. To my disappointment, this New York office was very parochial with an undertone of competition that kept most relationships at arm's length, especially if you were an outsider like I was. My willingness to be vulnerable was blunted by my need to be protective and my awareness that not everyone there wanted to either help me succeed or collaborate. There were exceptions, and those friendships where I set down my general wariness are the ones that remain to this day. Interestingly enough, the person I became closest to was my immediate superior. We had many opportunities to discuss the issues of the department and ideas for improvement. More importantly, I felt able to let my guard down with him and be more vulnerable. I am convinced that this very act of exposure allowed us to become close friends, which we remained until his untimely passing.

There are instances when you may feel the need to be more protective. But I'm confident it's not in as many situations as we may think. When I look back, I understand why I closed off, and at the same time I see that I could have done it less.

Some of the best models of vulnerability I've seen in my

CONNECTABILITY

professional life were two men named Mitch and Frank. I sat next to Mitch for fifteen years. Mitch wasn't the usual Wall Street type, but he was the best relationship salesman I have had the pleasure of working with. In the savage, insular New York atmosphere, he was never truly given credit for his accomplishments nor for his ability to build relationships. Regardless of how he was viewed within the firm, his clients loved him. The relationships he built stood the test of time. To this day, Mitch has access to his previous clients, as he built relationships that had a certain amount of vulnerability. He not only built credibility as an accurate source of information but also shared enough of himself to reach beyond the transactional. He was and is authentic.

I also worked with a man named Frank whom I didn't know as well but knew enough to be impressed with how far his client relationships exceeded the merely transactional. He possessed a rough and private exterior with his colleagues at the firm, but he was willing to expose his vulnerable side to his clients. These client relationships were deep, highly personal, and long-lasting and touched on all aspects of his life.

I bring these two men as examples of how business relationships don't always have to be siloed into numbers and transactions or conversations around what you did over the weekend. There's room for all of this, but you can stretch beyond these limits, too. Mitch and Frank are examples of how to build long-term, enduring relationships that can enrich your life even beyond your time in the office.

As I think back on my relationships that have stood the

Vulnerability

test of time, I realize they all have a commonality: I allowed myself to be vulnerable in them—not from a point of weakness but from a point of honesty and availability. I brought my authentic self. Admittedly, the topic of vulnerability is truly against the grain from what we have been traditionally taught as the way to perform in our jobs, especially when they're highly competitive ones. That model would have us remain guarded and protective. Don't give up too much information about your clients. Show toughness at all costs so you're not taken advantage of. Everything is transactional, with a winner and a loser. Those people with whom you have ongoing, rich exchanges are relationships where you have shared some degree of vulnerability. This brings them depth and mutual satisfaction. The vulnerability of mutual discovery lays the framework.

Daniel Simons and Christopher Chabris designed a selective attention test to show how we focus our attention. In this video test, the viewer is asked to count the number of times a basketball is passed between players wearing white T-shirts. During the test, a person dressed in a gorilla suit walks through the players. Strikingly, most viewers fail to even notice the gorilla.[3]

This test illustrates how when we are paying very close attention to one task, we often fail to notice other essential ones. I like to think bringing our vulnerable self is the gorilla that we miss in relationship building. We are so focused on making the sale or even our relationship-building goals, we often miss the very thing that almost always helps deepen relationships.

CONNECTABILITY

The desire to not expose oneself is understandable, but limiting. For the richest business relationships and the richest life possible, we need to move beyond our reservations and embrace vulnerability.

CHAPTER 11
Bringing It All Together

We've spent the last chapters talking about ten essential human qualities that we each have developed to greater and lesser degrees throughout our lives. They are each powerful in their own right in the realm of relationship building. As powerful as they are individually, they become extraordinarily effective when used together. They are needed in this digital world, more than ever. This book is a reminder to not leave your humanity aside—if you want to build quality relationships.

CONNECTABILITY

I would like to offer a way to put some of these ideas together around three basic, minimum goals that are part of a valuable, successful relationship. We can call them the three C's: connection, converting, and concluding.

It starts with connection. You cannot build a relationship unless you first discover a reason to connect, a purpose that is of mutual benefit to you and the person with whom you are building a relationship.

Years ago, during the beginning of rapid media and technological growth, the head of the investment banking division at Goldman was concerned the firm had no relationship with a growing media empire located in Southeast Asia. So he set about to change that by somehow bringing about that all-important first meeting. It would not be easy and took some creative thinking. He needed to connect first, otherwise no relationship could be built. Sometimes that is easy, as the potential individual is ready to connect. However, more often than not, some creative thinking is required to secure that first opportunity to connect.

So the head of the banking division devised a clever way to create that first meeting. It turned out the owner of this media company took the same commercial flight between Australia and NYC every month. He probably would not do that today—he'd fly privately—but it was a different time when the world was more trusting. One thing that would remain the same? This man would still be the one you needed to talk to. He was important.

The head of the investment banking division was important too, but he was having trouble connecting in a traditional

Bringing It All Together

manner. The potential client believed he did not need the services of Goldman, and so, as company folklore has it, the investment banker had to stretch his thinking: How can I connect with this person? How can I think outside of the traditional silos of introductions?

He was creative, and, bound by fewer security restrictions than we have today, he came up with a plan to gain a first meeting. Once the banker learned that the prospect took the same flight every month between NYC and Sydney, he managed to get himself on the same flight and in the first-class seat right next to the media company owner. By the time the sixteen-hour flight concluded, he had succeeded: A first meeting was arranged. Of course, there was more to do from there. The relationship required follow-up and further care. But it began during that flight, and over time would prove to be a very successful relationship for both parties.

I believe this is a true story from the firm's history, but regardless of the accuracy of exact details, the story points out the need for and benefit of creativity in forging that initial connection. Creativity is a vital part of relationships at every stage, but I'd like to note its additional value in gaining that connection in the first place.

You have to first meet and connect before you have anything at all to work with. Ideally, who do we most want to connect with? Important people. The boss usually decides. It happens that they can be some of the hardest to reach, which is why creativity can be an incredible tool in putting yourself in the best possible position. Another vital piece

CONNECTABILITY

here is that you need to view yourself as important too. Being in that mindset will fuel your ability to connect, because important people like to talk to other important people. Don't underestimate what you bring to the table for them.

The risk of spontaneity with a bit of a chameleon will help you to be someone who can blend and adapt in varying situations. It is not dishonesty; it is about being flexible. When we're overly rigid in our beliefs, we automatically limit ourselves to certain possibilities. Spontaneity and adaptability are relationship development assets, and so these abilities are worth developing.

Every relationship has to have a starting point, which means finding the reason for connection is your first goal. To build that foundation, do your due diligence, gain knowledge, and develop an understanding of your clients' needs. After you've established those needs, then you prepare to solve for those needs using the tools we have been discussing. A good business plan or a good outline is always a strong start, and today, we have a surplus of digital and analog tools that can support us.

There are a wealth of digital tools to track and maintain information that will help you prepare and organize your meetings. It bears repeating—the digital tools of today help us track and remember when in-person communication is needed. The human voice is still the most powerful, especially when it's coming to you from right across the table.

Once you've connected, remember that the next goal is simply to connect again. It's not time to focus on selling anything. The goal is to obtain a second meeting and

Bringing It All Together

let things develop, using your attention to focus on these human-powered elements.

Once you secure a second meeting and both find value in continuing the relationship, then you can begin to promote yourself or your product. As you begin to develop this relationship, you will move into another stage: the time to convert.

I've come to realize that in any relationship there is the ability to sell an idea or a value proposition. It's just a part of life; we are all selling when we are interacting with another human. And when we have the ability to convince another of the value of our thoughts and ideas, we succeed in sales.

Being successful in this stage draws upon and brings together everything we've talked about in this book. If you can bring together empathy, listening, passion, risk, creativity and knowledge, being present and available, leadership, generosity, follow-up, and vulnerability, you're going to be excellent at converting in your sales work.

Converting is just another way of saying convincing, and it holds power in all areas of your life. In our personal interactions, we want to convince others that we are worth their time to get to know. If we want to build a new relationship, we want them to be convinced of the same, creating a chance to develop what can bring additional value to each of our lives. A successful relationship will be your ability to convert it to a place of growth and stability.

Convincing and converting sound like I am trying to move you to a place you do not want to be—there can be

CONNECTABILITY

a negative connotation to the words. Yet there shouldn't be. Convincing is simply the ability to convert another to your way of thinking. It is your ability to reach a place of understanding. To help another understand what you have is of value. It's acknowledging that we usually have a preference and would like others to align with the outcome we're hoping for, if possible.

We are so trained to think of sales in the negative. Think of these common phrases: "He sold you on a bill of goods" or "You were really sold." These imply that by selling, I got away with something. I would suggest that you instead view selling as having a conversation that can add value. Before converting and convincing, you have ideally listened and understood what the relationship needs. Through this positive framework, you are able to reach a beneficial outcome for both parties. In my work in sales, I always saw the long-term rather than the short-term gratification of making a sale. Bringing satisfaction to both parties, not just one, was essential.

An example of mutual satisfaction took place when I was the chairman of a university foundation board. There are many such boards around the country, created to further connect the universities with the communities in which they operate and to encourage financial support for the institutions. My vice chair and I believed that this particular university needed to improve its marketing so it would be easier to raise money. Universities often see themselves as educational centers that benefit the community, and the idea of "advertising" seems a little too secular. They feel their

Bringing It All Together

achievements should be enough of an incentive to garner additional contributions from alumni and the community. My co-chair and I understood their discomfort but felt a change in approach was still needed.

We were charged with convincing and converting the deans of the university to understand the value of our proposal. We took the time to understand the deans' point of view. Then we spent time educating them on how our idea was not to diminish the university in any way but to enhance. Our goals were in complete alignment although our methods differed, and once we realized our shared values, we were able to find common ground through a foundation of trust. The deans decided to hire a firm to help develop a more cohesive representation for the entire university. This approach not only benefited the branding of the university but also helped our fundraising. It stands as a good example of convincing and converting, seen through a positive framework.

From here, we move to concluding, or closing, as is the more common expression. The ability to close and conclude is believed to be the end result of developing a successful relationship. We often hear the description of a good salesperson centered solely on their ability to ask for the order and close. That is a shallow description, though, because like with our personal relationships, we want to develop relationships that are of long-term value beyond any one transaction. Situations change, and business is dynamic. We need relationships that are adaptable. Concluding is not an end of one sale but reaching a true empathetic understanding of our value system and the client's. This is a conclusion we can build on.

Remember, we can't always control the outcome of our efforts. What we can control is our efforts to do the right thing for ourselves and our clients. Our dedication to the values we have been exploring will create the best possible outcome, again and again. When thinking of concluding, be patient. You may not always make the sale when you want to, but you will make it when your client wants it.

My work with horses has underscored this truth for me. As we have discussed in earlier chapters, I have learned a great deal about patience in my work training horses, as well as about what I could control and not control. In the beginning, my goal was to win an event, and I felt I was doing all the correct things to achieve this goal. However, like in any goal-oriented relationship, the goal itself was not always in my control. And it was many years before I actually achieved a win. Patience played a large part in my eventual success. When I ultimately achieved my goal, it was exhilarating.

While the language of concluding sounds as if it brings with it a final end point, that's not the reality in a successful relationship. We don't want to finish it. We want it to grow. There is nothing more satisfying than a connection that moves from one successful outcome to the next. Always ask questions and seek to discover more about the relationship you are developing.

As you move through these three core stages of sales development—connect, convert, and conclude—remember

Bringing It All Together

all of the human-centered building blocks we've been talking about. When you bring everything together, you develop relationships with lasting positive outcomes.

Now I'd like to look at these ten elements working together through a different lens, by returning to a relationship that was career changing for me, my relationship with the Kamehameha Schools Bishop Estate.

The account was principally a fixed-income investor. We started our relationship at a time when interest rates were high, unlike more recent times when interest rates were exceedingly low. The bond market provided securities with fixed coupons and thus fixed rates of return. This market allowed the estate to better plan with a reliable revenue stream.

The estate's principal business, however, was real estate, and the beneficiary of this business was the Kamehameha Schools. When I agreed to cover this account, I was intrigued by its deep history interwoven with the history of the State of Hawaii. After researching and gaining a deeper understanding of the account and the culture around it, I began calling on their treasurer. Over the course of the years of coverage and visitation to the account, I was introduced to the five trustees. The governing board members of the institution are appointed by the Hawaiian Supreme Court. This board made all important decisions for the trust. I came to know the hierarchy of the organization, and through those contacts and my growing knowledge, I was able to learn their needs and present positive solutions. The relationship that was developed was a collaborative one

CONNECTABILITY

with shared information and mutually beneficial results. Working with all levels of the organization created trust and understanding. This level of understanding can only come from consistent communication.

In the early nineties, the investment banking world was changing, as markets were larger and risk more complicated. Most of the bulge bracket firms were publicly traded. Merrill had gone public in 1971, Morgan Stanley in 1986, and Shearson American Express spun off Lehman Brothers in 1994. Goldman chose to remain a private partnership but was interested in acquiring more capital in the early nineties.

At that time, the firm decided that becoming a public company was not in the best interest of the partnership. However, they did decide to seek other sources of capital in order to compete with the other publicly traded firms. Specific requirements were established for a transaction to take place. Significantly, it had to be funded with long-term capital, and the investing unit could not be involved operationally with Goldman. These limitations made the available potential investor universe very small.

I was aware of Goldman's capital requirements and the criteria for such an investment. I felt an investment like this would be beneficial for the Kamehameha Schools. Although they would be a limited partner, it would give them access to the expertise of what was arguably the premier investment bank in the world. I called Goldman's treasurer who was in charge of the project and explained to him who my client was and why this would be a good fit. Although unaware of the account and its heritage, he

Bringing It All Together

nonetheless agreed that I could show the potential transaction to the chairman of the Bishop board.

I then called the chairman of the trust at home to set the stage for a high-level call. I explained the firm was interested in raising additional capital. The terms of the investment were relatively simple: $250 million invested, a long-term investment without maturity, and a limited partnership structure. I told him he would have access to the firm's substantial knowledge, advice, and resources. There was a brief pause while he thought about what I was offering. To this day, I am somewhat struck by his accepting the terms so quickly. I explained that I did not have the authority to affirm the transaction. We would have to fly to New York and meet with the senior partners, as they would have the final word. He understood, and we agreed to leave for New York the next day.

By the time we began discussing this transaction, we had built a relationship over twelve years. Within a few days the chairman and I were sitting in a conference room with the senior partners of the firm in charge of this large transaction. The group was led by the head of the fixed-income division, who would become the senior partner in two years.

Once we had agreed to the broad outline of terms, a term sheet was prepared for signatures. The Goldman and Kamehameha representatives were chatting after the meeting. The Goldman rep was explaining that there would be a due diligence period for the estate to understand the business they were investing in. He went on to explain that since I was not a partner, I would not be permitted to be a part of these meetings. At this, the Kamehameha chairman responded that if I were not in the meetings, he would not be attending either. It was an incredible affirmation of our relationship and the trust that had been built up over the years. The firm found a way around this requirement and I was included, and the transaction was concluded about a month later. The Kamehameha Schools Bishop Estate became only the second outside investor in a partnership that was established in 1869. Two years later, the Bishop Estate would invest an additional $250 million. This was again an affirmation of the relationship and trust that had been built over the years.

This was a watershed event in my career with the firm, and for me it serves as an example of the principles I have come to recognize as these ten key, foundational tenets of relationship building that draw upon human connectivity. Here is how I would summarize how they each contributed to a transaction built around trust:

1. **Empathy.** *Taking the time to understand your client is the foundation of developing a trusted working relationship.* At the core of this story is the knowledge built around a sincere interest in the organization and the people responsible for its operation. I had a good historical background and developed an empathetic understanding of Hawaiian history and of this organization. My story with the Bishop Estate is about caring for others—being interested in building a body of

Bringing It All Together

knowledge that would help us know each other better, thus achieving a value proposition for both parties. The story of the Hawaiian people is closely linked with the Bishop Estate. Princess Pauahi was the last remaining relative of the great King Kamehameha who united the Hawaiian Islands. The estate is also an organization linked with development from outsiders that came in large part at the expense of the Native Hawaiians. Understanding the nuances of an organization, as well as cultural suspicions around it, becomes valuable information as one builds an intimate business relationship. Take the time to empathetically understand your client and the people with whom you are building relationships. The more you understand, the more you will be able to gain and build trust.

2. **Listening.** *In the arena of sales, you cannot be the center of attention.* If you are doing all the talking, you are not learning anything and you are not listening. Your ability to be empathetic allows you to demonstrate that you care to know. The key to active listening is the ability to ask relevant questions. Not only will you find shared commonality but you will also learn valuable information, which will help form the basis for future transactions. Peeling back the layers of another person or organization is the fun part of

relationship discovery. Over years of interacting with the Bishop Estate, I learned about the organization and the goals and culture that drove their decision-making. Through active listening, I learned what would be most valuable to them and how this large transaction could help them.

3. **Passion.** *If you are passionate and knowledgeable, you will remove the skepticism one might naturally have with a new idea.* If you do not believe in yourself and your ideas, how can you expect me to believe? The power of passion will allow your knowledge and enthusiasm to strengthen your ability to convince others. My relationship with the Bishop Estate carried a quality of aliveness in it from the start because of my passion for my work. As I learned more about the culture of the Hawaiian people and the uniqueness of this institution, my passion grew. My enthusiasm and interest became obvious to my client, who grew in confidence and trust that I could bring the best the firm could offer.

4. **Risk.** *In order to build a solid relationship, you will have to risk the possibility of being rejected.* Through empathy, listening, and passion, you will build the confidence to take the risk to connect with people and build successful relationships. Every time you send a text, pick up the phone, or meet with someone in person, you are taking

Bringing It All Together

a risk. With the Bishop Estate, I took a risk in first accepting such a client, dedicating time and energy, and taking a risk with a creative idea. They were not known by the firm and were not a known commodity in the world of large, capitalized institutions. I was their representative at the firm, and so I took on risk they might not be the type of institution that the firm would want to partner with. As it turned out, the risk I took to represent them as the best candidate for a limited partnership was a risk worth taking for both. It involved putting my own personal capital at risk to achieve an outcome that was of value to me, the firm, and our client.

5. **Creativity and knowledge.** *Creativity and knowledge help you contribute more than your competition.* The more knowledge you can accumulate on an organization and the people you will be in relationship with, the more valuable you become to yourself and your client. You must continue to be interested in learning more. Every organization is a dynamic one, and thus the need to stay knowledgeable will demonstrate your interest. Developing creative solutions to problems will come from understanding and knowledge. They were not the most likely candidate to be issuing commercial paper as an educational institution. Similarly,

they were not the obvious choice for seeking a large amount of capital. However, through knowledge and understanding, they were deemed the perfect partner.

6. **Being present and available.** *Open to the pleasures and opportunities of the moment.* Every job and every day present a litany of challenges. However, those challenges become far worse if you do not enjoy what you are doing. One way to find greater joy in your work is opening to what the moment presents you. What can you find in it? I found reward in many things, but especially from working with my clients. Their success was a greater reward. By opening up so fully to my relationship with my clients, we developed a level of loyalty and trust that brought us each great success.

7. **Leadership.** *Leadership comes from knowing what is needed and executing it in a shared effort.* It comes from setting the best course and guiding others through your actions. It comes from acting as a steward for something greater. Anyone can be a leader. With the Kamehameha Schools Bishop Estate, I didn't simply follow a previously set path. I forged a new one. They were not the obvious choice, but they developed into a trusted partner. I like to think that leadership takes a certain amount of risk, but it also requires a good amount

Bringing It All Together

of confidence you are doing the right thing. If you lead with confidence, you are doing the right thing for your client and the firm, and it increases the chance for a positive outcome.

8. **Generosity.** *Generosity is sincerity and openness; it is not a transaction.* Being kind and generous of spirit goes far toward building a long-term, collaborative relationship. I was generous with my time and interest with the Bishop Estate for years, and so was the firm. One interesting side note concerning the Bishop Estate's investment in Goldman is not only was the Bishop Estate investing in Goldman, but Goldman was also investing in the estate, whose sole purpose is to educate Hawaiian children through the Kamehameha Schools. At the end of this transaction, the firm established two scholarships to help graduates with tuitions at universities on the mainland. This was generosity in a way many of us see generosity. But I see it as more than that. It was an act that showed the estate the firm was interested in more than just their investment—it also understood the importance of education and the importance of helping underrepresented children. It was generosity of spirit.

9. **Follow-up.** *Following up is a simple, critical part of developing relationships.* The extraordinary effort you make to stay in contact will be

of infinite value. During the Bishop Estate transaction, the amount of follow-up needed was immense. From meetings with department heads to gathering the information needed for thoughtful analysis, this transaction and its follow-up items stretched in every direction. If there were negotiation challenges, those had to be resolved quickly or the transaction would not have moved forward. I had to demonstrate that the Bishop Estate was of the highest priority, and one way of doing that was to follow up promptly on all items that arose during the daily due diligence meetings. If you want to demonstrate your commitment to the qualities discussed in this book, make sure you follow up on all tasks, simple and complex. Sometimes the simplest detail can sidetrack or derail a valuable project.

10. **Vulnerability.** *You can't do great things without risking rejection.* In many relationships, opening up your authentic self is what allows you to build deeper bonds. As I said in the beginning of this book, there is nothing more satisfying than a relationship that moves from one successful outcome to the next. In many ways that is how my relationship with the Bishop Estate grew, as we explored new ways to access the capital markets. As I look back, I see how the client and I developed a level of vulnerability that drew us

Bringing It All Together

closer together. The honest dialogue between us kept the transaction on track when there were times it was at risk. The willingness to expose myself to criticism or to stand firm on issues of importance proved to be the catalyst to such a positive outcome. We were true friends, but we also represented institutions we had sworn to support and do our best for. Being vulnerable allowed us to each occupy both of these spaces and achieve great success. When it came down to it, this investment was built around trust.

My work with this account took place in an environment that didn't have the same number of digital tools we do today. The same principles that were essential then would be equally essential now. You just can't reach people in the same way unless you meet them on a human level.

This was made crystal clear when I recently attended a board meeting where the CEO made a strong impression on me (and the others in the room). He talked about his vision, and as he did, we could hear the power and belief in his voice. He became emotional, and that emotion underscored how much he cared. He was so enthusiastic about what he was describing, what he was building, and his vision for the future.

Before seeing this man in person, I'd been familiar with him from a digital distance. When I was in his presence, I realized he was a sincere and effective leader. As he

CONNECTABILITY

shared his vision, I could feel the strength of his leadership. As I listened to him speak, he exemplified the power of human connectivity.

With digital communication, information is understood in black and white. Our brains aren't built for electronic signals, and when our communication is primarily based on digital means, we can't feel the energy in an exchange. As we use the growing digital tools available, it's essential we continue to cultivate the qualities in ourselves that will allow the greatest human connection.

None of these qualities are rocket science. It's easy to agree that they are beneficial and something to aspire to. So why did I feel the need to write this book? While we may all recognize these qualities are valuable, we don't see them as cornerstones to building success in sales and our relationships. We need to do the work of growing them into a discipline and ritual that are part of our effort.

With this book, I want to underscore the importance of these qualities, bring awareness to their role in building relationships, help you realize you can grow in these areas, and help light a fire under you to take a disciplined approach to doing just that.

This isn't a how-to book; it's an awareness book. If you want to build solid, deep relationships that let you achieve great success, you can. Your most valuable tool kit comes from within; you just need to access it. In other words, cultivate your skill with these tools through awareness, intention, and a regular discipline that brings your attention to them with consistency.

Bringing It All Together

When I speak of discipline, I don't mean just pushing yourself to do something. I mean a daily routine that brings these elements together so they become second nature. Approach these elements with a sense of ritual and devotion.

Rituals are an important part of our lives. They can be as simple as setting a consistent time to eat dinner or setting the intention to always eat dinner as a family. Ritual gives us stability and dependability. It can help us cultivate new habits.

That's the challenge of these qualities. The challenge, once you have the awareness around them, is in living them out. It's like making a baby; getting started is the easy part, but until you hold one in your arms, you never fully understand the journey you're going to embark on. And while learning from others about how to care for a baby is important, it's going to be harder to actually do it than read about it. That's probably the same for any undertaking, and it's no different with what I'm suggesting. Deepening our abilities in these skills of human connectivity is a lifelong practice, and I hope I've convinced you it's a worthy apprenticeship.

Through the combination of analog and digital, we can achieve greater success in sales and the further development of enduring and meaningful relationships. The digital universe will keep on evolving, and more devices and platforms will be created to help make us be more efficient and connected around the world. Regardless of the tools we will build, we cannot change that we are human beings who strive to be connected in a meaningful way with other

CONNECTABILITY

human beings. Humanness can't be replaced by a machine. It's the most valuable quality we can share with others. More than any digital tool, personal care is what will grow our business relationships in a far deeper way.

My hope is this book will serve as a reminder and help you achieve great success in both your work and your life.

Afterthought Number 1

In writing this book, I interviewed several people connected to the story. In doing so, I discovered some interesting links between my early Wall Street days and my interest in restaurants, which illustrate the power of human connective skills across industries.

In 1989, my first boss in the trading and investment world, Malcolm Skall, retired from A. G. Becker, which had been merged with Merrill Lynch. His wife, Nancy, had always wanted to live on a farm. Malcolm, though, had no experience with physical labor. Born in Cleveland and

CONNECTABILITY

raised on the Chicago Board of Trade, he knew who to call when things broke down. The idea of doing it himself was not in his wheelhouse. Furthermore, the idea of growing and harvesting produce was definitely not his idea of retirement. But he was a loving husband and he also knew how to sell and build relationships. The two of them decided to buy an eight-acre treasure in Healdsburg, California, where he and Nancy proceeded to develop the established Middleton Farm.

The town of Healdsburg in Sonoma County is the central town of the agricultural region north of San Francisco. It is often linked to the more "bougie" wine region of Napa and its central town of St. Helena. Yet while Healdsburg is a town noted for wine, it's more known for agricultural products and an important farmers market. Under the stewardship of Malcolm and Nancy, Middleton Farms grew in reputation to become the gold standard for local produce, becoming a central figure in the growing farm-to-table cuisine that would come to dominate restaurants in California.

Middleton's impressive reputation came about in large part through Nancy's green thumb and the practices they used to grow their produce. For example, their strawberries are considered by many the most delicious in California, with seeds that somehow magically arrived from France. But their success and golden reputation were also due to Malcolm, who remained forever the quintessential salesman. After he and Nancy embarked on their new adventure, he took the relationship development principles and skills he'd developed over a life on Wall Street and leveraged them to

Afterthought Number 1

help make his wife's dream come true. It was Malcolm who sold the product and developed the relationships, including those with leading California icons of the food-to-table movement Alice Waters and Thomas Keller.

Malcolm was known for walking into Keller's restaurant The French Laundry to deliver produce before then asking for a sandwich. It was his wit and personality that also helped bring people to his vegetable stand, despite the high prices. He remembered names and important events and built a loyal following. Years after his time on Wall Street, he was still a dedicated relationship builder. After his passing, Nancy carried on the tradition of what they had created until her death. Middleton Farm, under a different name and family, still continues to this day.

Three hundred miles away and years later, Daisy and Greg Ryan, the owners of Bell's, were developing their own relationship with an equally excellent and proficient small farm in the Santa Ynez Valley, Finley Farms. Building a Michelin Star restaurant requires the highest-quality ingredients, and Bell's has built its reputation around the best of both service and product. Finley Farms is noted for providing excellent produce. What they do not have is a salesman in the Malcolm Skall mode, but they have built deep relationships with the local community and restaurants. I also discovered that Daisy and Greg are connected to the Thomas Keller network of fine restaurants and superior chefs, with both of them having spent time working in Keller restaurants and Daisy often still invited as a guest chef for special events. Today, Daisy's daily routine is to

CONNECTABILITY

shop at Finley Farms with her son, Henry, to pick the fresh produce that will feature in the evening creations at Bell's.

These stories are linked in the obvious—food and restaurants—but to me they are also linked through people connecting authentically. Malcolm's way of connecting with others contributed to his and Nancy's success in a completely new endeavor, and Daisy and Greg's way of taking time to connect daily with the individuals growing food for their restaurant leads to the finest food and an impeccable dining experience. Daisy isn't placing a produce order electronically and waiting for it to arrive. She's engaging face-to-face, which helps her and Greg create something of the highest excellence.

The digitalization of our day-to-day life has been firmly established and its usefulness embraced by all of us. However, the creation of long-lasting successful relationships—ones that can build a farm business and grow its reputation, lead to Michelin Star–quality products, or, for all of us, create a life rich in professional success and personal satisfaction—comes from our paying attention to the human connective skills we all possess but sometimes forget to bring into sharper, deeper focus.

These skills are worth remembering. They're worth cultivating. And if you agree, I hope you devote yourself to this journey and experience its great rewards.

Afterthought Number 2

The skills we have been discussing are important on their own, but they are most effective in combination. When building relationships, we tend to focus on the singular target. However, like many things, "it takes a village," as the saying goes. In addition to the human qualities we have been discussing, it's most important to be aware that the circumstances and people around you can be instrumental in building a successful relationship. What follows is a story of overcoming distance, circumstance, and profession to build a rewarding relationship—with an assist from coincidence.

CONNECTABILITY

Lyle Lovett is, among many other things, a brilliant, accomplished musician and songwriter. His music genres include country, rock, R&B, big band, and beyond. He performs with some of the best musicians, as they all desire to play with him. The University of California at Santa Barbara has an Arts and Lectures program that is second to none. It has been led for many years by Celesta Billeci. She provided the venue and circumstance that allowed me to first meet Lyle Lovett. Remember that often the people you least expect may provide the conduit to meaningful relationships.

Lyle Lovett first came to UC Santa Barbara to perform twenty years ago. I was invited backstage to meet him. He noticed my boots and said, "Where did you get those boots?" He knew my boots were made by Lee Miller of Texas Traditions, as he, too, was a client. That moment discovering a common interest led to the further discovery of other mutual interests. Lee Miller himself, in the same way as Celesta, became a common thread that allowed our relationship to flourish.

Lee Miller was the apprentice and heir designate to Charles "Charlie" Russell Dunn (c.1898–September 23, 1993), the quintessential American bootmaker of hand-made Western and cowboy boots. Lee and his wife, Carrlyn, have continued the tradition of Charlie Dunn in the same building under the name Texas Traditions. I was introduced to Carrlyn and Lee many years ago. In a similar fashion to the work of Lyle Lovett, their product is a true work of art and artistry.

Afterthought Number 2

Relationship building is often the result of many threads rather than one. Lyle and I were brought together by unplanned circumstances and common acquaintances. Despite distance, occupation, and background, Lyle and I were introduced to each other through the thoughtfulness of other people. Once we discovered the commonality of our interests, the foundation had been laid, and we made the effort to help it grow. Being present allows you to take advantage of opportunities that may arise to deepen a relationship.

On this particular occasion, I had come to Austin to meet with my publisher to launch *Connectability*. I was going to meet with Lyle and Lee for different reasons. I needed Lee to adjust a pair of boots, and Lyle and I were going to meet at the conclusion of his recent tour. I felt this was an opportunity for the three of us to be together in the same city. We met at the Texas Traditions workplace, where we spent a couple hours talking about boots and horses. At one point Lyle asked what I was doing for lunch. I said I was open, and we agreed to meet at a restaurant in Austin.

I stayed behind to continue my conversation with Lee about some boot repair. As it happened, Lee and I started talking about legacy and what each of us would want to leave behind. Coincidentally, later at lunch, Lyle and I started talking about the same thing, maybe because we were all three humbled by the realization that there is less time in front of us than in back. But that day we were not dwelling on that. Instead, we chose to fully appreciate the gift of our relationship.

CONNECTABILITY

Connectability is all about the skills that will reward you with the kind of relationships that will better you as a person and allow your life to be richer beyond the transactional. This story of four people seemingly disconnected by geography, background, and vocation demonstrates the unique human quality of building relationships. It represents the unique confluence of passion, empathy, knowledge, vulnerability, and follow-up.

We become vulnerable and present when we venture out of our comfort zone. Lee is a quiet artisan who spends most of his time with a small circle of people, all of whom are involved with the skill of making his intricate boots. The fact that Lee would make himself vulnerable to step out of his comfort zone circle of colleagues to communicate with me demonstrates a desire and ability to be vulnerable. Lee demonstrates this when he calls me both to check in as a friend and also to see if I am having any boot issues.

Lyle Lovett spends a great deal of his time in the music world. Therefore, stepping out of that world to spend time with somebody like me, who is not a musician and not an artist, demonstrates a certain amount of vulnerability.

Again, in a similar way, I am also doing the same thing. So the three of us each have a skill set, but that skill set does not intertwine with the others'. Therefore, we have all demonstrated that the desire to be friends is greater than the desire to be comfortable. This is what I mean by being vulnerable.

The three of us will continue to benefit from the awareness that we each must make the effort to stay connected.

Afterthought Number 2

Remember that following up is your responsibility, your legacy, and your gift to the relationships that you have built. It is never too late to pick up the phone or write that letter. Your relationship is waiting for that effort. Lyle, Lee, and I live miles apart and have different jobs, but the fabric of our lives is forever enriched by the effort that we have made for each other. The next rich encounter is just ahead, and we are ready.

This concludes my book-writing effort. The following lyrics are from a favorite Lyle Lovett song. It seems appropriate for this book, as we are at "Closing Time."

Closing time
Unplug them people
And send them home
It's closing time
The night's all that's left behind
You take your part and I'll take mine
And go on home
It's closing time

—*Lyle Pearce Lovett*

Thank you very much.

Notes

Introduction

1. "Zoom Conversations Suppress Brain Activity, Yale Study Finds," News Medical Life Sciences, October 25, 2023, https://www.news-medical.net/news/20231025/Zoom-conversations-suppress-brain-activity-Yale-study-finds.aspx; Nan Zhao, Xian Zhang, J. Adam Noah, Mark Tiede, Joy Hirsch, "Separable Processes for Live 'In-Person' and Live 'Zoom-Like' Faces," *Imaging Neuroscience* 1 (2023): 1–17.
2. "Zoom Conversations Suppress Brain Activity."
3. Erin Blakemore, "'Zoom Fatigue' May Take Toll on the Brain and the Heart, Researchers Say," *The Washington Post*, November 25, 2023, https://www.washingtonpost.com/health/2023/11/25/zoom-fatigue-brain-heart-effects/.

CONNECTABILITY

4. "Workplace Skills Survey;" "Most Workers See Need for Greater Balance Between Tech and Human Skills: Deloitte Survey," Deloitte, October 21, 2024, https://www2.deloitte.com/us/en/pages/about-deloitte/articles/press-releases/most-workers-see-need-for-greater-balance-between-tech-and-human-skills-deloitte-survey.html.

Chapter 1

1. Christian Jarrett, "Why Are Humans So Curious?," BBC Science Focus, https://www.sciencefocus.com/the-human-body/why-are-humans-so-curious.

Chapter 3

1. The Britannica Dictionary, "passion," accessed February 6, 2025, https://www.britannica.com/dictionary/passion.

2. Andrea Hsu, "America, We Have a Problem. People Aren't Feeling Engaged with Their Work," NPR, January 25, 2023, https://www.npr.org/2023/01/25/1150816271/employee-engagement-gallup-survey-workers-hybrid-remote.

3. Jim Harter, "In New Workplace, U.S. Employee Engagement Stagnates," Gallup, January 23, 2024, https://www.gallup.com/workplace/608675/new-workplace-employee-engagement-stagnates.aspx.

4. Kris Paterson, "Are Work Friendships Becoming a Thing of the Past?," What News?, updated April 7, 2025, https://www.whatjobs.com/news/are-work-friendships-becoming-a-thing-of-the-past/.

Notes

Chapter 5

1. Adam Hayes, "Commercial Paper: Definition, Advantages, and Example," Investopedia, updated April 23, 2025, https://www.investopedia.com/terms/c/commercialpaper.asp.

Chapter 6

1. *State of the Global Workplace 2022 Report: The Voice of the World's Employees* (Gallup, 2022), 2, 6.

Chapter 9

1. Brian Williams, "21 Mind-Blowing Sales Stats," Brevet, https://blog.thebrevetgroup.com/21-mind-blowing-sales-stats.

Chapter 10

1. Thesaurus.com, "vulnerable," acccessed July 18, 2025, https://www.thesaurus.com/browse/vulnerable.
2. Subscription to my blog available at www.fredricsteck.com.
3. Daniel Simons, "But Did You See the Gorilla? The Problem With Inattentional Blindness," *Smithsonian*, September 2012, https://www.smithsonianmag.com/science-nature/but-did-you-see-the-gorilla-the-problem-with-inattentional-blindness-17339778/.

About the Author

Human connection has defined every chapter of Fredric Steck's forty-year career in financial services, from his beginnings at Goldman Sachs to becoming a pre-IPO partner at the firm. Today, as an author, speaker, and consultant, Fred helps salespeople and development officers connect to clients with authenticity and humanity in a digital world. Inspired by both professional work and personal passions, Fred infuses his writing with wisdom, wit, humanity, and honest experience.

Fred has advised and served on the boards of the UCSB Foundation, the Buck Institute, Aravo Solutions, and Thorne/DNP. He has also given workshops and keynotes to organizations such as Share Our Strength, University of Denver, University of California at Santa Barbara,

CONNECTABILITY

Washington State University, Cal Poly State University, and the Commonwealth Club.

To learn more about Fred and his work, please visit www.fredricsteck.com.

Acknowledgments

"You should write a book."

It seems easy enough to do, but like most things, it is harder than you think. This project has been one of the most difficult things I've ever done, but it would never have happened without the support and kindness of many people.

I am sending a massive thanks to Stacy Ennis, book strategist and coach. She is everything I am not; she is detailed and exact about her craft. It was her attention to detail—along with her artistry—that gave me the support and courage to write *Connectability*. In addition to giving me her guidance on every detail, she introduced me to Robin Bethel, my editor. Editors are not people who correct syntax;

CONNECTABILITY

they are true partners in writing. Robin encouraged me to bring my most authentic self to this process and insisted that my heartfelt commentary belonged in every chapter. These two women spent hours working with me. Their kindness, patience, and sincerity were central to my effort and their encouragement kept me going.

Books need publishers, and I want to thank mine. Greenleaf Book Group took the chance to publish an unknown author in a very competitive space. Thank you to the Greenleaf team, including Justin Branch, Sally Garland, Jamie White, Kristine Peyre-Ferry, Gwen Cunningham, Adrianna Hernandez, and the other fine professionals who all contributed to making this a successful and well-crafted book. I am grateful for your dedication and expertise in bringing this work to fruition.

I had the option of picking a "safe" cover design. It was the clever Jonathan Lewis who came up with the idea of the book's cover. I am appreciative of his artistic talent and his thoughtful connection to my book.

Thank you also to Nour Seikaly, who has taught me that public relations are a good thing. She was the first "outsider" to read the manuscript and acknowledge its value. Her firm, Grey House, has managed to bring this project to the attention of those I hope will benefit from its message. I have been so appreciative and beyond impressed with her level of focus and creativity throughout this process.

Thank you to all those mentors along the way—Malcolm Skall , John Farmer, Mike Mortara, Billy Shore, Matuo Takabuki, Oz Stender, Chris Norton, Jeff Flug, Mike

Acknowledgments

Zamkow, El Gray, Tom Triggs, and many others who as friends and colleagues have encouraged me on many levels—and at times of difficulty. Their friendship and our relationship form the basis of my belief in the positive nature of connection.

Thank you to all of the readers of my blog "È Solo Un Trucco." Especially my most loyal commentator, Kat Porter-Steck. Your many complimentary messages on my blog posts encouraged me to keep writing, explore my artistry, and to find my voice in the written word. In the end, your encouragement of my writing instilled the confidence in me to take on this project.

Thank you to Daisy and Greg Ryan, Nancy Oaks, Danny Meyer, Monica Torggler, Alessandro Montagna, and all those who work tirelessly in the kitchen to produce a hospitality experience that reminds us of the very humanness of breaking bread together and experiencing what is uniquely human—connectability.

Thank you Rocket, Smarty, Cindy, and all those magnificent horses who taught me patience and understanding and the ability to communicate on the most basic level.

Grazie mille—Teresiana Matarrese e Linda Riolo—I miei insegnanti di italiano. Connectability does not only exist in English. You have taught me the importance of language in different forms and especially the most beautiful language—*Italiano*.

With love for my parents, who—as parents should, but many do not—encouraged me to pursue life with enthusiasm and a positive view of life's challenges. My father was